John Henry Cornell, Ludwig Bussler

The Theory and Practice of Musical Form

John Henry Cornell, Ludwig Bussler

The Theory and Practice of Musical Form

ISBN/EAN: 9783337379698

Printed in Europe, USA, Canada, Australia, Japan

Cover: Foto ©Thomas Meinert / pixelio.de

More available books at **www.hansebooks.com**

THE

THEORY AND PRACTICE

OF

MUSICAL FORM:

ON THE BASIS OF

LUDWIG BUSSLER'S

"MUSIKALISCHE FORMENLEHRE."

FOR INSTRUCTION IN COMPOSITION BOTH IN PRIVATE AND IN CLASSES

BY

J. H. CORNELL.

NEW YORK: G. SCHIRMER, INC.

PREFACE.

FORM, in art, may be comprehensively defined as the external shape and order in which artistic conceptions are presented,—in other words, as the outward expression of the subject-matter or import of the art-work. Accordingly, there may be as many forms as art-works, although numbers of these individual forms may and actually do agree in certain essential features. Now, the summary of the principal features in which a number of art-works agree, is called Art-form.

The necessity of form to the special art of music is, perhaps, not so immediately obvious as in the case of the other arts; yet it is certain that without an adherence to the laws of form a coherent, intelligible musical composition is as inconceivable as—for example—a picture, a sculpture, or a building, without plan or design. A piece of music (if indeed music it should be called) without a determinate tonality or key-relationship, without harmonic, melodic, rhythmic order and symmetry—in a word, without *form*,—is nothing else than a tonal chaos. Hence the absolute necessity to the would-be musical composer of the study of the laws of musical form,—a necessity from which no natural gifts, not even the possession of genius, can dispense him. "Form,"—says ECKERMANN (Beiträge zur Poesie)—" is the result of the efforts, through thousands of years, of the most excellent masters, which every one cannot too soon appropriate to himself. It were a most insane delusion of misconceived originality, if each one were to go about on his own account fumbling for that which is already on hand in great perfection. Form is handed down, learned, imitated, otherwise progress in art would be out of the question,—every one would have to begin anew," etc., etc. And GOETHE, speaking of the strict requirements of the laws of art-form, says that it is " precisely genius, natural talent, that is the first to understand them, and that pays them the readiest obedience." The study of musical form, however, of course presupposes the knowledge of the laws of *Harmony* and *Counterpoint*, as an indispensable preliminary condition; which knowledge, accordingly, is in this work assumed as part of the student's equipment.

In view of the fact that the *means* or *organs* by which musical tones are produced are either *natural* (the human voice), or *artificial* (musical instruments), music is either 1. purely VOCAL; or, 2. purely INSTRUMENTAL; or, 3. MIXED—*i. e.*, at once *vocal and instrumental*. To one or the other of these three grand divisions of musical forms every musical composition must be assigned. Further, each one of these form-genera, as embracing compositions having either but *a single movement*, or *many movements*, is, accordingly, either SIMPLE, or COMPOSITE (CYCLICAL).

Again, each one of the three form-genera has its various SPECIES, as follow.—**A**. VOCAL FORMS.—(a) For a *solo voice*: Recitative, Air, Arioso, Arietta, Ballad, Canzone, Canzonetta, Cavatina, Romance, Song, Scena, etc.—(b) For *several solo voices :* Duet, Terzet (Trio), Quartet, Quintet, Sextet, etc.—(c) For *chorus a cappella* (with or without solo): Chorus, Mass, Psalm, Madrigal, Motet, Glee, etc.—**B**. INSTRUMENTAL FORMS. (a) In *one movement* (*simple*): the various Dances and Marches; Pianoforte pieces, such as Etude, Song without words, Fantasia, Nocturne, etc; Orchestral Overture (Opera-overture, Concert-overture), etc.—(b) With *many movements* (*Cyclical*): Duo, Trio, Quatuor, Sextet, Septuor, etc.; Concerto, Suite, Serenata, Sonata, Symphony, etc.—**C**. MIXED VOCAL AND INSTRUMENTAL FORMS. (a) The various *choral compositions* with organ or orchestral accompaniment, viz.: Mass, Litany, Te Deum laudamus,

Stabat Mater, Service, Anthem, Hymn, Psalm, Choral, Cantata, Oratorio, Passion, etc.—(b) Represented on the *Stage:* Opera, Operetta, Melodrama, Vaudeville, etc.

The forms chiefly treated of in this book, as constituting the basis of the greater part of the instrumental compositions of HAYDN, MOZART, BEETHOVEN, WEBER, SCHUBERT, MENDELSSOHN, SCHUMANN, etc., and of most living composers, are called the FORMS OF INSTRUMENTAL MUSIC. Here music is free from external restraints (such as are imposed by the *text*, etc., in *vocal* music), and rules according to the laws of its own nature. The influence of these forms, however, on vocal music—especially that of the above-mentioned composers—is great, and easy of demonstration.

The present book is substantially a translation of LUDWIG BUSSLER'S "Musikalische Formenlehre," a work much to be recommended for its clearness and thoroughness, to which, in its present English dress, I have made considerable additions. Within the last few years much has undeniably been done in our country (thanks to the greater number of thorough and conscientious teachers) in the direction of a more solid musical education; and among other results, the importance of the subject of musical form is beginning to be appreciated, not only by the professional student of music but also by the rapidly increasing class of advanced amateurs desirous of an *intelligent* enjoyment of the masterpieces of composition. The present addition to the meagre vernacular literature of the subject will therefore, as I hope and believe, be welcomed by all interested in the cause of this beautiful art.

The *aim* of the work is, in one word, to teach *musical construction*, and its *plan* is perfectly simple. Each form, beginning with the very smallest of the elementary ones, is clearly explained and copiously exemplified; the student is then required to originate a musical thought in the given form. As repeatedly stated in the Exercises, the first compositions—those of small extent—are to be utilized for constructing the succeeding ones, of larger form; this will facilitate class-instruction in musical form, as but few pupils are able to continually furnish new material for these Exercises without becoming superficial and careless.

For valuable matter gathered for this book from GROVE's Dictionary, DR. STAINER's "Composition," ARREY VON DOMMER's "Musikalisches Lexicon," F. J. KUNKEL's "Melodiebildungslehre," BENEDICT WIDMANN's "Formenlehre," HERRMANN KÜSTER's "Populäre Vorträge," etc., I hereby acknowledge my obligations.

J. H. CORNELL.

NEW YORK, JANUARY, 1883.

CONTENTS.

FIRST PART.
THE ELEMENTS OF MUSICAL FORM.

FIRST DIVISION.
THE SECTION AND PHRASE.

SECOND DIVISION.
THE PERIOD.

THIRD DIVISION.

THE SMALL PRIMARY FORMS.

FOURTH DIVISION.

THE LARGE PRIMARY FORMS.

CHAPTER XVIII.

CHAPTER XIX.

CHAPTER XX.

SECOND PART.

APPLICATIONS OF THE PRIMARY FORM.

FIRST DIVISION.

COMPOSITE PRIMARY FORM.

CHAPTER XXI.

CHAPTER XXII.

CHAPTER XXIII.

CHAPTER XXIV.

CHAPTER XXV.

SECOND DIVISION.

THE LOWER RONDO-FORMS.

CHAPTER XXVI.

CHAPTER XXVII.

CHAPTER XXVIII.

CHAPTER XXIX.

CHAPTER XXX.

THIRD DIVISION.

CHAPTER XXXI.

THIRD PART.
THE SONATA-FORM.

FOURTH PART.

THE HIGHER RONDO-FORMS.

APPENDIX.

FIRST PART.

THE ELEMENTS OF MUSICAL FORM.

FIRST DIVISION.

THE SECTION AND PHRASE.

CHAPTER I. (Introductory.)

METER. RHYTHM.

1. METER, in music, is the grouping of two, three or more tones, as time-units, into a whole, or time-integer, called *Measure*, the first part of which—the <u>*Thesis*</u>—has an accent, the second part—<u>*Arsis*</u>—(♪ either no accent or a weak one. Thus, the grouping, *e. g.*, of four quarter-notes into a measure gives the meter whose signature is $\frac{4}{4}$, the principal accent being on the first quarter-note, the weak (secondary) accent on the third : $\frac{4}{4}$ ♩ ♩ ♩ ♩ . In a piece of music, embracing a series of measures, the *rule* is that all measures have (1) the *same number* of time-units (metrical parts) of *equal length* ; and (2) a *uniform* alternation of *accent* and *non-accent* ; *i. e.*, the accent falls on the same metrical part in one measure as in another. The regularly recurring accent enables the *ear* to separate the measures one from another; for the *eye*, they are separated by means of the vertical line, called *bar*.

2. RHYTHM has regard to the motion of tones on the basis of metrical division and comprises (1) the combination of tones of equal or of unequal duration (represented by the various kinds of musical notes) into manifold small time-figures, forming distinct groups (in this sense every germinal musical thought—or, technically speaking, *Motive*, consisting of a few notes, or of notes and rests, and more or less sharply outlined by means of a cæsura,* is *a rhythm*) ; (2) the combination of these smaller rhythms into larger forms—Periods, etc., in which larger sense the word rhythm expresses the *grouping of measures*.

3. For the sake of convenient reference, rhythms are designated according to the number of measures they occupy. Thus we have the *one*-measure rhythm, or MONOMETER ; the rhythm of *two* measures—DIMETER; of *three* measures—TRIMETER; of *four* measures—TETRAMETER ; of *five* measures—PENTAMETER, etc. The measures are of course counted from bar to bar, when the rhythm begins (whether with a note or a rest) at the very *beginning of the measure ;* otherwise the ear counts the measure from the *first tone to the completion of the value of the measure* (this is indicated in many of our illustrations by the bracket ⌐⎯⎤). In the latter case the rhythm is said to begin on the ANACRUSIS,† of which our illustrations afford many examples.

---

* The Cæsura, or point of division, marks the *rhythmical* end-point of both the larger and smaller parts of a melody. As the cæsura is not always the *final note* of a part of a melody, it should be distinguished from the "Section" and "Phrase," terms which indicate the small portions of a melody with regard to their *melodic* end-points. The cæsura always falls on an *accented* metrical part.

† A Greek word borrowed from poetry and suggested instead of "Up-beat" (from the German "Auftakt"). The Anacrusis is essentially the beginning on a non-accent or a weak accent. Hence, in duple, quadruple and triple meter,—assuming that the metrical parts are *quarters*, and overlooking for the present the metrical *members* (divisions of the quarters into eighths, sixteenths, etc.), the following anacruses are possible: (1) in $\frac{2}{4}$ only one : ; (2) in $\frac{4}{4}$ *three*, viz: a) ; b) ; and c) taking as anacrusis the third quarter, with *secondary* accent: ; (3) in $\frac{3}{4}$ *two :* a) ; b) Moreover (to speak now of the smaller divisions of the measure), the unaccented *members*—not only of the unaccented but also of the *accented* metrical parts afford anacruses, thus greatly increasing their number. Here are some examples in $\frac{2}{4}$ of anacruses afforded (1) by members of the arsis: (2) by members of the thesis: The application to still smaller members (*e. g.*, etc.), and to triple and quadruple meter offers no difficulty. Here follow a few

4. The Monometer sometimes occurs as rhythmical unit, in *immediate repetition*, as in the following example:*

it is, however, generally combined with another—larger—rhythm, either **(a)** *preceding* it, as in the following example, in which the two monometers are followed by a two-measure rhythm (dimeter);

or, **(b)** *following* it, as:

or, finally **(c)** inserted *between two larger rhythms*, as:

examples of anacruses in *compound* meter, say $\frac{6}{8}$:

* The quotations are given mostly in a melodic abridgment, for saving room.

5. The monometer consists generally of but *one* tone-figure. Thus, in Fig. 1, measures 1, 2, we have this principal rhythmic figure:

; in Fig. 2, measures 1, 2, the figure : in Fig. 3, measures 2–4, . The larger rhythms, on the contrary, are generally composed of many, for the most part different, tone-figures, as for instance in Fig. 4, measures 1–4 ;

this tetrameter is therefore a *composite* rhythm, comprising four different tone-figures.

6. The most common constituent of melody is the *rhythm of two measures*—dimeter, which we shall therefore assume as the starting-point of formal construction.

CHAPTER II.

SECTION.

7. To render the meter of a musical thought intelligible to the *ear*, it is requisite that this thought *exceed the limit of one measure*. For, it is only by the recurrence of the same elements of the meter (the same metrical parts) in the second measure, that the meter can be recognized by the hearing.

8. A tone-succession which, extending beyond the limits of one measure, renders the meter recognizable by the ear, is called in general a PHRASE, specifically a SECTION, when its usual extent is that of *two measures*. The section, in this sense, constitutes the fundamental element of our classical instrumental forms, collectively, so that the greater part of the compositions in these forms can easily be divided up into sections.

9. We distinguish *three kinds* of sections, viz : (a) that which *quite fills—with tones—*the space of two measures, as:

(b) that which *does not fill out the second measure* with *tones,* but either supplements it with *rests ;* as,

or, leaves the remainder of it free, for the introduction of a new thought; as,

(c) that which *leads over into what follows* (the third measure); as,

10. Many sections are formed by the *repetition of a one-measure thought* (monometer); as,

The repetition need not, however, be as *exact* as in the above examples; it may embrace only the essential *rhythm*, while admitting *tonal variations;* as,

In referring, when desirable, to this construction, it will be expressed by the metrical cipher 2 × 1.

11. It may be observed here, that there will occasionally be found

portions of the measure, the section, etc., consisting mostly of figures not strictly belonging to the essential rhythm, but merely serving to connect two rhythms, which figures, or (as they sometimes are) single notes, may be called MELODIC CONJUNCTIONS. These are indicated in the following examples by brackets:

FIRST EXERCISE.

Compose many sections of all the three kinds, especially of the first.

These sections should be arranged with complete harmonization for the piano (some, at option, for string-quartet, organ, as also for voices), the best ones to be selected, and, with a view to future use, *numbered*. The principal *tempi* to be indicated. Here follow three examples from BEETHOVEN, one of each kind:

MODELS.

c. *Adagio grazioso.*

CHAPTER III.

DOUBLE SECTION.   PHRASE.

12. The mere *repetition* of a Section (dimeter) does not constitute a *4-measure phrase* (tetrameter); it is simply a DOUBLE-SECTION, indicated by the cipher 2×2.

13.

Among these repetitions are included—as in the case of the construction marked 2×1 (see Chap. II, Paragraph 10), such *variations* as are of a *tonal* (not rhythmical) nature; but even here there must be a perceptible similarity, in spite of the variation, as in the following examples:

14.

Even *rhythmical* variations are admissible, if confined to *subordinate details*, as is the case with embellishments, figurations, etc.

15.

(The + in the above two examples calls attention to the slight rhythmical changes introduced in the repetition, in Ex. **a**, by the insertion of a changing-note, in **b**, by the omission of the anacrusis.)

13. A musical thought forming a *section* sometimes occurs *four times* in immediate succession. Such a construction, embracing eight measures, is called QUADRUPLE SECTION, and marked 4 × 2. For an example see Fig. 263.

14. Every extension of a musical thought to *four measures*, other than any such extension already noticed, constitutes the PHRASE, or Tetrameter. This too, like the section, is either (**a**) *filled out*, or (**b**) *disjunct*, or (**c**) *connective*,—each of these terms referring to the construction of the second constituent section.

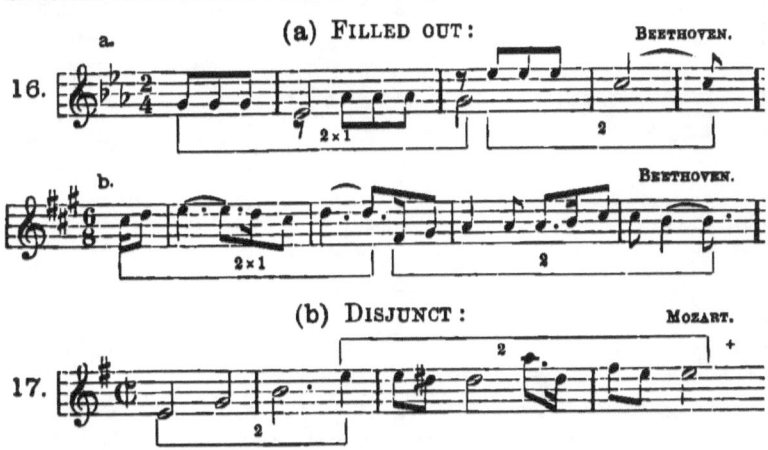

(At + a quarter-note of the measure remains free, serving as a starting-point for a new thought.)

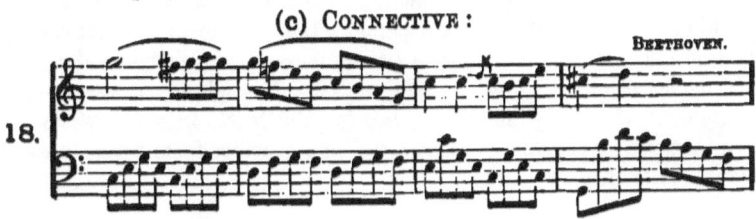

SECOND EXERCISE.

Compose very many 4-measure phrases, (1) by completing the NUM-
BERED sections composed for the first exercise, each one in a different
manner; and (2) NEW ones.

MODELS.

15. The form of the phrase just considered is perhaps the com-
monest, yet it is not the only one.   The truth is that the structure of
the phrase does not absolutely depend on the number of four measures,
for there are phrases of as few as *two* measures (these occur chiefly in
the *compound meters*) and as many as *ten*.   The phrase is essentially
an element of melody embracing *two* (at the least) *or more* measures
terminated by a *cadence* of some kind, and sensibly forming a separate
group by itself.

REMARK.—The doctrine of the *harmonic close*, or *Cadence*, may here bo succinctly stated. The Cadence, strictly so-called, is that whose final harmony is the *Tonic Triad*. If this Triad is immediately preceded by the *dominant* harmony, we have tne *authentic* tonic cadence ; if by the *subdominant*, the *plagal* cadence, or *tonic half-cadence*. The authentic tonic cadence is *perfect*, when the uppermost tone of the final chord is precisely the *tonic itself, i. e.,* not its *Third* nor its *Fifth ;* in either of the latter cases the cadence is *imperfect*. Another kind of cadence, improperly so called, consists of a point of rest on the *dominant* harmony, generally preceded by the tonic Triad. The expression *half-cadence* (when the word " tonic " is not prefixed) designates this point of rest on the dominant, indicated in some of our illustrations by I V, or ι V. The abbreviations " Per. Cad." (perfect cadence) and " Im. Cad." (imperfect cadence) refer of course to the authentic tonic cadence, whether the tonic of the key of the piece be meant, or the tonic *for the time being,* resulting from a *modulation.*

16. The phrase is *simple,* if consisting of *but one rhythm,* and *composite,* if embracing more than one rhythm. Every simple phrase is therefore a rhythm, but not every rhythm is a phrase, because in many rhythms—especially the smaller ones—both the extent of at least two measures and the cadence are lacking.

17. At the close of most initial phrases of a melody, the ear expects a second phrase of analogous rhythmic structure, as complementary or responsive. This expectation is generally fulfilled, for, in fact, phrases are most frequently paired in this way, as we shall see farther on. Nevertheless, the phrase beginning a melody occasionally ends with a *perfect authentic tonic cadence,* thus forming a musical thought which is in so far satisfactory in itself as it does not so imperatively require a subsequent phrase as complementary. As a general rule, a phrase, or larger group, closing with a perfect authentic cadence on the tonic of the key, is regarded as *absolutely independent and complete in itself,* and may be followed, at pleasure, by a heterogeneous group, or by a repetition, etc.

18. Here follow some examples of phrases outside of the regular form of four measures. They are given for promoting the insight into the nature of the phrase, not for imitation at the present stage of our study.

TWO-MEASURE PHRASE.

(Other examples of the 2-measure phrase, Fig. 33.)

FIVE-MEASURE PHRASE.

SIX-MEASURE PHRASE.

SEVEN-MEASURE PHRASE.

TEN-MEASURE PHRASE.

BEETHOVEN.

REMARK.—The last example, Fig. 24. illustrates the *independent tonic ohrase* spoken of in Par. 17. The *eight-measure* phrase will be considered later.

SECOND DIVISION.

THE PERIOD.

CHAPTER IV.

THE SIMPLE, EIGHT-MEASURE PERIOD.

19. The PERIOD is a tone-form outlined and organized in a certain rhythmic, melodic and harmonic order, constituting in itself a little piece of music, or forming in conjunction with other periods a member of a larger composition. We are speaking of the period with special reference to the free forms of *instrumental* music, as distinguished from *vocal* music, in which latter its laws are more or less conditionated by the text.

20. The period, in its typical and most usual form, consists of *two four-measure phrases*, the first being generally called *Thesis*, the second *Antithesis*. This is the *simple* period. It closes mostly with a *tonic cadence;* a different close, as for instance in the key of the *dominant,* or—in minor—in the *parallel major key*, of course presupposes either a repetition of the period itself, closing this time in the tonic, or the addition of other periods.

21. As to the *tonal contents* of the period, the general rule and practice is that of *similarity* in the two phrases. This is not essential, however, as the Antithesis often shows a construction differing from that of the Thesis. What is generally essential is, that there should be a certain *contrast* between the two phrases, whereby the second one may appear as complementary or *responsive* to the first (see Par. 17). This is usually effected by the harmonic *cadence*.

22. The repetition, without material alteration, of a *phrase*, constitutes simply a DOUBLE-PHRASE, marked, in metrical cipher, 2 × 4.

23. But if the repeated phrase contains certain changes whereby it is *harmonically contrasted* with the first one, so that the two phrases are correlated as Thesis and Antithesis, we have the PERIOD.

This correlation is based on the different ways in which the two phrases *close*. Hence result *four different forms*.

FIRST FORM.

24. The *Thesis* closes with a *half-cadence*, the *Antithesis* with a *perfect authentic cadence in the tonic*.

THIRD EXERCISE (1).

Compose many eight-measure Periods of the first form, some new, others extensions of former exercises.

MODELS.

SECOND FORM.

25. The Thesis closes with an *authentic cadence* in the DOMINANT.

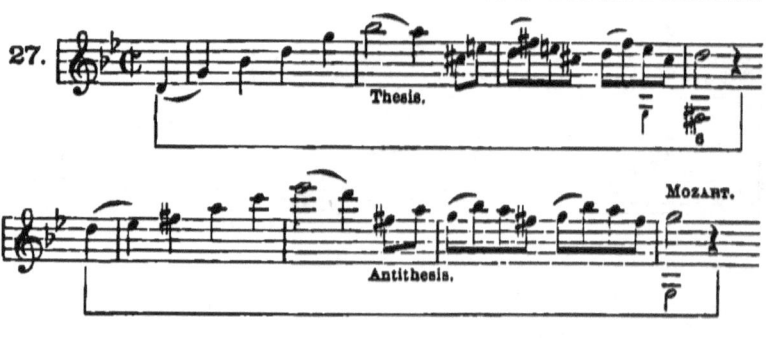

THIRD EXERCISE (2).

Compose many Periods of the second form, partly by varying exercises written in the first form.

MODELS.

BEETHOVEN.

b. *Allegro molto.*

THIRD FORM.

26. The Thesis closes with an *imperfect*—exceptionally with a *perfect*—*authentic cadence* on the *Tonic*.

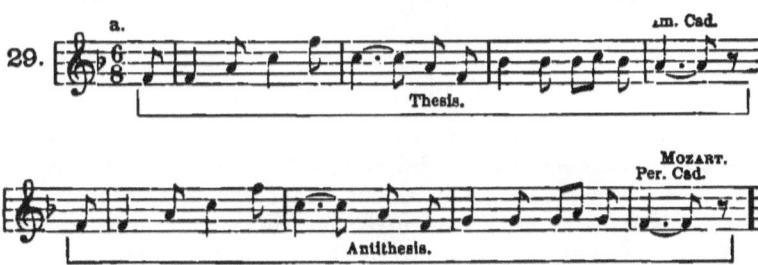

THIRD EXERCISE (3).

Compose Periods in the third form.

MODEL.

FOURTH FORM.

27. In the three period-forms which we have thus far considered, the two phrases show a decided *similarity* as to tonal contents, the Antithesis being to a certain extent a repetition of the Thesis. In the *fourth* form the Antithesis corresponds only *approximately* to the Thesis, sometimes even is constructed from motives quite different from those of the Thesis, thereby showing a *thematic* contrast, in addition to the contrast afforded by the harmonic cadences.

THIRD EXERCISE (4).

Compose Periods in the fourth form.

CHAPTER V.

EXCEPTIONAL PERIOD-FORMS.

FOUR-MEASURE PERIODS.

28. The Period, as thus far exemplified, has invariably exhibited a specific *symmetry*, in the grouping of its phrases by 4 measures, or by 2 (4+4, or 2+2). Periods in which this symmetry is lacking will now be illustrated.

SIX-MEASURE PERIODS.

SEVEN-MEASURE PERIODS.

EIGHT-MEASURE PERIOD.

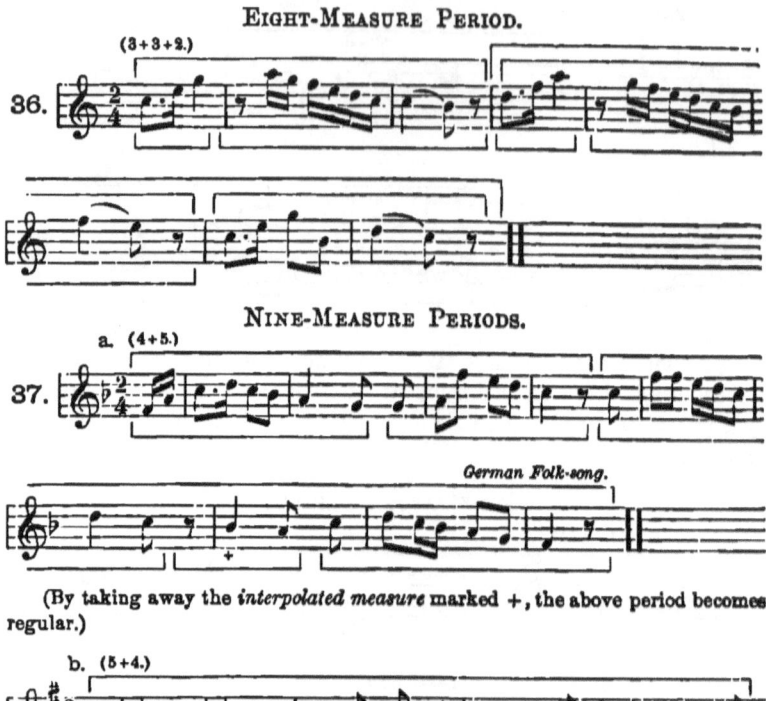

NINE-MEASURE PERIODS.

(By taking away the *interpolated measure* marked +, the above period becomes regular.)

TEN-MEASURE PERIODS.

(In Fig. 38 a, the melody really ends with the first half of the eighth measure, the two remaining measures forming a *Coda*, so called. This is a common construction.)

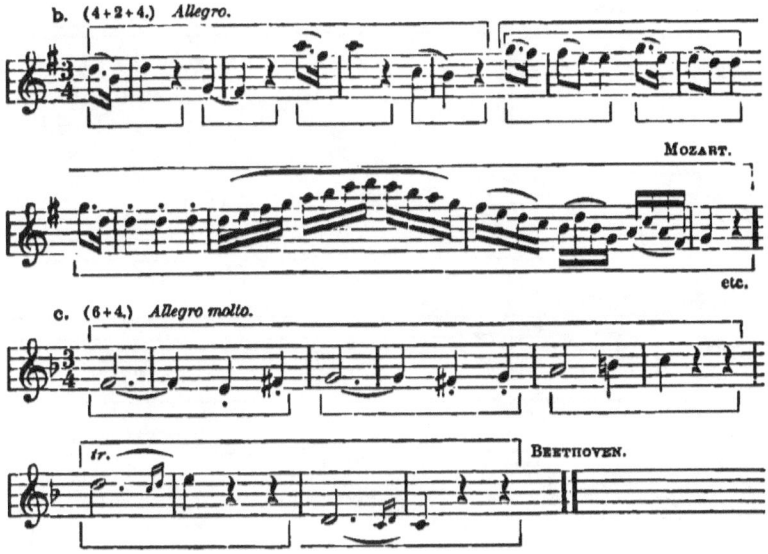

PERIODS OF THREE PHRASES.

29. Periods of *three phrases* are often found, having of course for the most part *twelve measures*, sometimes more, sometimes fewer. Such a period is not unfrequently composed of a Thesis and a *double Antithesis*, or vice versa, of a *Double Thesis* and an Antithesis. In other cases the second phrase does not form part of the Thesis or of the Antithesis, but appears simply as *middle phrase*.

c. 12 Measures (3 × 4).

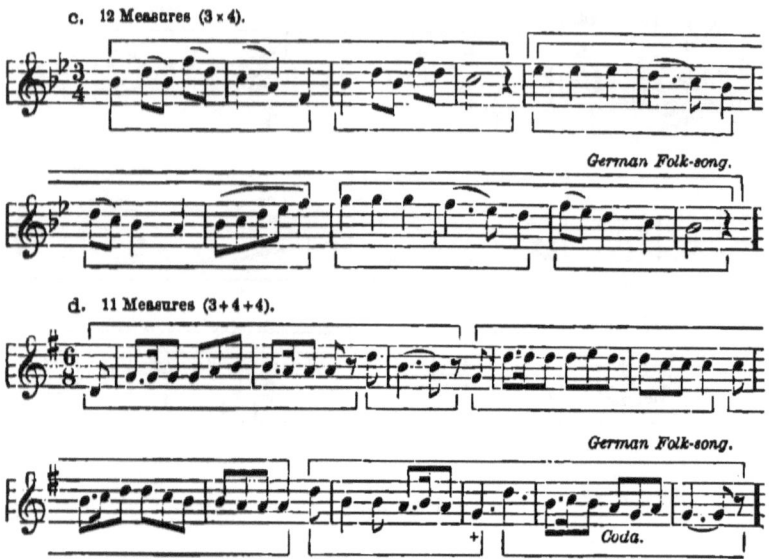

German Folk-song.

d. 11 Measures (3 + 4 + 4).

German Folk-song.

Coda.

(The above melody, Fig. 39 d, really ends on the note marked +, what follows is virtually a repetition, as it were a Coda.)

e. 13 Measures (4 + 2 + 2 + 5).

NÄGELI.

30. The young composer who here applies to the study of the musical forms, will, over and above the working out of his exercises, carefully notice all the forms which he meets with in his daily musical life, always explaining them to himself according to the doctrine of form. It may also be assumed that he carries in his memory a treasure of classical music, from which he can draw models for every form, without having to consult scores. Every species of music in which our masters have composed, affords abundant material for this, not only instrumental but also vocal music, opera and oratorio.

THIRD DIVISION.

THE SMALL PRIMARY FORMS.

CHAPTER VI.

THE SMALL TWO-PART PRIMARY FORM.

31. The mere *repetition of a period*, even with modifications, does not give rise to a higher form. But the union of two periods so constructed that one constitutes a *Thesis*, the other its *Antithesis*, affords the TWO-PART PRIMARY FORM. This is the simplest of all musical forms after the period, being almost synonymous with " tune," " melody." In this form were cast the first beginnings of melody, especially the typical folk-song, called by the Germans " Volks-lied," from which circumstance some musical theorists of that nationality have called the form " Lied-form," the English equivalent of which is "song-form." But as this form embraces a great many different species of music-pieces, such as the various Dances and Marches, the Theme with variations, etc., etc., the name *primary form* has been suggested* as more appropriate to it. The essential principle of the primary form is the presentation of one musical thought (or of one *principal* thought), followed by another, contrasting with it, then returning to the original to conclude.

32. A general rule for the structure of the two periods is, that the Thesis of the *second* one is formed of *new matter*, whilst the Antithesis (of the same period) exactly corresponds to the Antithesis of the *first*.

FIRST FORM.

33. The 1st period is precisely of the kind described in paragraph 24 and exemplified in Figs. 25, 26. The periods composed for the

---

* By a writer (Mr. C. H. H. Parry) in Grove's Dictionary of Music and Musicians. His article, under the title " Lied-form," is well worth reading.

Third Exercise (1), page 29, should here be utilized. In the 2d period, the *Thesis,* whose matter more or less differs from that of the 1st period, closes with the *Half-cadence,* and, exceptionally, with one of the cadences mentioned in Chapter IV, paragraphs 25, 26. *Antithesis* exactly corresponds to that of the 1st period.

FOURTH EXERCISE (1).

Compose, in accordance with the foregoing, very many small two-part primary forms, partly from the periods of the preceding exercise, partly from new material.

MODEL.

REMARK, as to Fig. 41. Here, as in many cases, the Antithesis of the 2d period is merely *similar*—not strictly corresponding—to that of the 1st period.

In a manner similar to the above, BEETHOVEN works up the period (*poco allegretto*) given in Fig. 26 b, into a piece in two-part primary form, in his Sonata, Op. 7, last movement. The Rondos in the two little Sonatas, Op. 49, also begin in this form.

SECOND FORM.

(1) IN THE MAJOR MODE.

34. The 1st period closes with an *authentic cadence* in the key of the *dominant*, implying a *modulation*. The 2d period is constructed as in the first form, and closes in the tonic. Occasionally, the 1st period closes with an authentic cadence in the (minor) key of the *Mediant* (for instance, in *e*-minor, if the major key be *C*, etc.).

FOURTH EXERCISE (2).

Compose small pieces in major, in the second two-part primary form.

MODELS.

(2) IN THE MINOR MODE.

35. In minor, the 1st period closes either in the normal (minor) key of the *dominant* (for instance, *e*-minor, dominant of *a*-minor, etc.), or in the *parallel major* key (*C*-major, for instance, parallel major of *a*-minor, etc.).

MODELS.

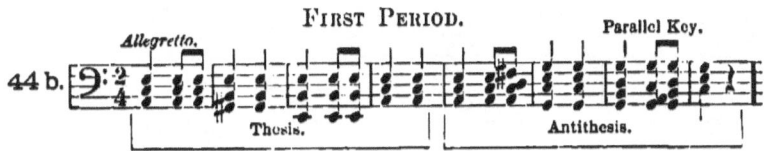

FIRST PERIOD.

SECOND PERIOD.

So, too, the melody which immediately follows the above, as a counterpoint to it, viz:

FOURTH EXERCISE (3).

Compose pieces in two-part primary form, in minor.

36. The repetition of a period, even with variations, yet *without the contrast* necessary for correlating the two periods as Thesis and Antithesis, as just illustrated, constitutes simply a DOUBLE-PERIOD, not a primary form. Thus, for example, the Scherzo of BEETHOVEN'S $A\flat$ Sonata, Op. 26, begins with an 8-measure period, which is immediately repeated with rhythmical variations.

46.

Such repetitions often occur in cyclical compositions, and should be well distinguished from higher forms. The *Allegretto* of BEETHOVEN's c♯-minor Sonata, Op. 27, also shows a similar repetition, written out, varied by ties, and rhythmically elaborated.

47.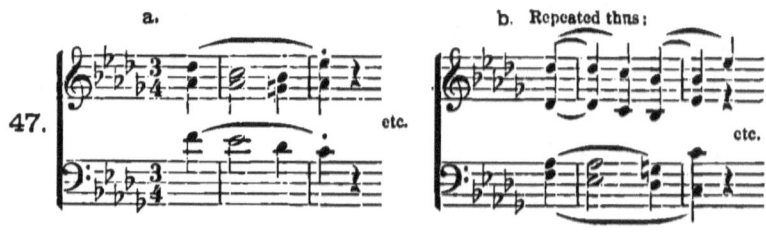

THIRD FORM.

37. It will be noticed that in the case of a repeated period like those in Figs. 46, 47 there is no harmonic correspondence of the cadences, *i. e.*, the cadence of the second period does not *contrast* this period with the first one, for the simple reason that each period closes with *one and the same* (the tonic) *cadence.* The case often occurs, however, of two connected periods almost exactly alike in which this harmonic correspondence of the cadences is found, whereby the two periods are made to correspond *on the whole* as Thesis and Antithesis, thus constituting a *third* two-part primary form. Examples of this are the two periods of the Rondo of BEETHOVEN's B♭-major Sonata, Op. 22, given below as a model (Fig. 48).

38. In such periods the Thesis of one corresponds to that of the other, the Antithesis of one to that of the other, unlike the first and second forms, in which Antithesis corresponds to Thesis. In this third form, therefore, Thesis and Antithesis usually have fewer features in common.   We may express the former relationship thus:

Thesis. Antith.   Thesis. Antith.
1st *Period.*   a   a   the present one thus: 1st *Period.*   a   b.
2d   "   b   a   2d   "   a   b.

MODEL.

48.

REMARK.—At the place marked + in the above example the amount of two measures (added in the original to the regular 8-measure form by a license to be explained later) has been purposely eliminated, in order that the example may serve as a model in the regular form. (See Fig. 67.)

FOURTH EXERCISE (4).

Compose pieces in two-part primary form with the construction just explained, and illustrated by the preceding model (Fig. 48).

CHAPTER VII.

THE LARGE (EIGHT-MEASURE) PHRASE.

39. Two connected phrases of different matter, yet without harmonic and rhythmic correspondence, form—not a *period*, but—an 8-MEASURE PHRASE. This construction may be regarded under three aspects.

(1) INDEPENDENT.

40. This kind of phrase is often *independent ;* in other words, is a musical thought forming a *complete whole in itself*, as closing with the *perfect tonic cadence* (see Par. 17).

Often the division into two parts is less obvious ; the phrase then seems to be simple rather than composite. For example :

50.

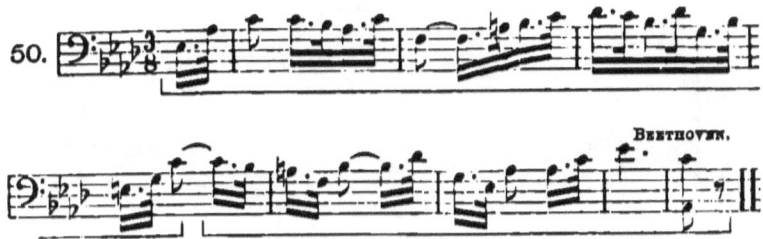

This construction may be considered the most perfect form of the phrase, and requires specially diligent practice.

FIFTH EXERCISE (1).

Compose many independent 8-measure phrases.

MODELS.

51 a.
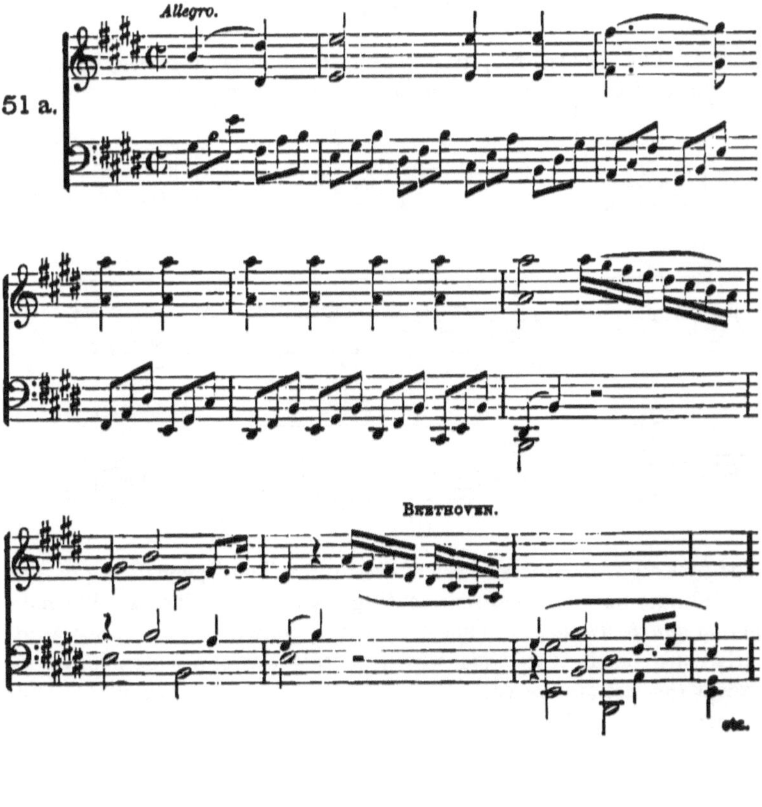

(2) As Part of a Period.

41. The 8-measure phrase may form *part of a period*, by taking the place of a *Thesis* or an *Antithesis*. For example:

The first eight measures of the above form a Thesis, consisting of two subordinate phrases, each representing a 4-measure Thesis. We have here a *double Thesis*, so to speak; to it is joined in this case a similarly constructed *Antithesis*, which repeats the entire double Thesis except the last two measures, in which it makes a *tonic cadence*. Thus is formed

The Large (Sixteen-measure) Period.

42. The above beginning of the *Allegro* of the *Don Giovanni* overture also forms a 16-MEASURE PERIOD, the first eight measures constituting the composite Thesis, the last eight the Antithesis.   By means of the lively rhythm of the close the period immediately connects with the succeeding one, a procedure which gives to the higher forms, especially in the *Allegro*, that quality of urging forward, that resoluteness, which constitutes their esthetic character.

43. *The large* (8-measure) *phrase may in all the higher forms occasionally take the place of the 8-measure period.*

FIFTH EXERCISE (2).

(**a**) *From the independent 8-measure phrases already written form 8-measure* THESES.

(**b**) *Develop these, by adding independent 8-measure phrases, into* 16-*MEASURE PERIODS.*

(**c**) *Compose* NEW 16-*measure periods, taking as models the examples already cited.*

(3) DOUBLE-PHRASE.

44. Likewise among the *phrases,* not among the periods, are classed those 8-measure constructions which, though they indeed show thematic correspondence, yet, by reason of perfect similarity of structure, in quick *tempo* convey the idea of *repetition* rather than of *period-form*.   Moreover, they form as a rule no complete cadences, though the contrary may obtain exceptionally.   We class these formations among the DOUBLE–PHRASES, without denying their relationship to the period.

MOZART was very partial to this construction, and used it in many of his finest compositions, but constantly treats it *as Thesis*, or even as *part* of a Thesis.   BEETHOVEN's *Egmont-overture* also begins with such a phrase.

Similarly constructed, but still more closely allied to the double-phrase, is the following Thesis of the *Pilgrims' Chorus* in *Tannhäuser*:

45. The character of mere repetition appears still more plainly when *both subordinate phrases* form *Half-cadences,* as in the following theme from MENDELSSOHN'S *a*-minor Symphony:

FIFTH EXERCISE (3).

Compose some phrases of this kind, after the foregoing models.

CHAPTER VIII.

THE LARGE THREE-PART PERIOD.

46. The LARGE THREE-PART PERIOD has the following construction:

> Thesis : 8 measures.
> Middle group : 8 measures.
> Antithesis : 8 measures.

This form sometimes takes the place of the small three-part *primary form.* It has no need of special practice. Here follows an example from one of MOZART'S early works; it contains, however, a small irregularity, viz., the *extension* of the second group to the length of *nine* measures, which will come under discussion later.

47. In most cases the large three-part period is regarded as a three-part primary form in which the period-form of the Thesis and Antithesis (first and third parts) is lacking, and large phrases take the place of 8-measure periods, which is *almost invariably* the case in the second part (middle group).

Examples of this species will be found in the exercises on the three-part primary form.

CHAPTER IX.

THE SMALL THREE-PART PRIMARY FORM.

48. The Three-part Primary Form is constructed by interpolating between the two divisions of the *third two-part primary form* (see Par. 37, 38) a division having the *same dimensions*. This added part is only exceptionally in *period-form*, having for the most part, for the sake of variety, any one of the 8-measure phrase forms (Chapter VII).

49. The three divisions of this primary form are severally named, according to their order,

FIRST PART,
SECOND PART,
THIRD PART.

In common parlance, however, the second and third parts are *classed together* as *Second Part*, because they are, as such, frequently repeated, and stand in common between signs of repetition. The following is the scheme.

FIRST PART.

50. THESIS closes with *Half-cadence ;* or, with the *imperfect—*

exceptionally the perfect—*authentic tonic cadence;* or, with *authentic cadence* in the key of the *dominant.*

ANTITHESIS closes (**a**) in *major :* in the *tonic;* or, in the key of the *dominant ;* or, in the key (minor) of the *mediant.*—(b) In *minor :* in the *tonic;* or, in the *normal* key (minor) of the *dominant ;* or, in the *parallel major* key.

THIRD PART.

51. THESIS closes just as in the first part, the Half-cadence predominating still more.

ANTITHESIS closes in the *tonic.*

REMARK.—The first and the third part may therefore under certain circumstances be exactly alike in construction.

52. Between these two divisions the three-part primary form interpolates a

SECOND PART,

of the same dimensions, which usually closes with a *Half-cadence,* in order to introduce the third part. This second part may be constructed out of new material, all the more so when there is great similarity between the first and the third part.

53. The application of the *large phrase-form* (Chapter VII), instead of the *period-form,* is feasible, not only in the second part (as already stated), but also in *each of the two other parts,* at pleasure.

SIXTH EXERCISE.

Compose pieces in small three-part primary form, partly from former exercises, partly of new material.

It will also be a very useful exercise to point out, in single one-voiced melodies, all the features of the formal construction here indicated.

MODELS.

* Here two measures are lacking, through abbreviation. See Chapter XIII. This license, however, should not yet be imitated here. Nevertheless, the example was chosen on account of the clearness of the construction of the second part.

FOURTH DIVISION.

THE LARGE PRIMARY FORMS.

CHAPTER X.

THE LARGE TWO-PART PRIMARY FORM.

54. Two 8-measure phrases combined form the 16-measure period (Par. 41), two 16-measure periods the 32-measure or LARGE PRIMARY FORM.

55. By repetition of the parts, whether they be repeated note for note, as indicated by the signs ‖: :‖, or whether they be varied and written out, the number of measures is increased to 64. Such a 64-measure primary form is for example the Trio in $D\flat$-major of BEETHOVEN's F-major Sonata, Op. 10, No. 2.

The variation, however, is limited here to the first part, whilst the second part,

60.

is *literally* repeated. The last six measures of the Trio do not belong to the form, but constitute an independent introduction to the following part, in *f*-minor:

61.

SEVENTH EXERCISE.

Compose pieces in two-part large primary form.

As model, take the Trio already quoted from the *F*-major Sonata; its insertion here, entire, would occupy too much space.

CHAPTER XI.

THE LARGE THREE-PART PRIMARY FORM.

56. As *two large* periods combined constitute the *two-part large* primary form, so the combination of *three* such periods gives the LARGE THREE-PART PRIMARY FORM.

57. The harmonic relations of the cadences of the parts, reciprocally, remain the same, as explained in Chapter IX.

58. In the ordinary Dance-forms (see Chapter XXII) the second period is commonly called *Second Part*, and forms, without thematic connection, generally a perfectly independent movement in the key of the dominant.

59. But when the second part is *thematically* connected with the first, it takes, seldom the form of the period, oftener that of connected phrases. This arises naturally from the necessity of different construction of the parts when there is thematic relationship.

60. This form is the predominant one among the primary forms. To it belong, for example, the greater number of the Minuets and Scherzos of the classical Symphonies, Quartets and Quintets, Sonatas for one or two instruments. Still the form is, in almost all these movements, by means of extensions and abbreviations, somewhat modified, though often quite immaterially. We give here, therefore, an example from a newer composer, the *Trio* from MENDELSSOHN's *A*-major Symphony, as showing exactly the division into three times sixteen measures, moreover as being worthy, in its subject-matter, of ranking with the classical masterpieces.

From this point on it is advisable to write the exercises for the *tring-quartet*, as piano-composition too easily leads to careless voice-*ending*.

EIGHTH EXERCISE.

Compose pieces in large three-part primary form.

FIFTH DIVISION.

LICENSES OF CONSTRUCTION.

CHAPTER XII.

EXTENSION.

61. Without its changing the form *on the whole*, the extension of part by an adjunct, called *Coda*, growing out of the context, is often net with. One of the simplest examples of this is the theme given in *Fig. 25 b*, from MOZART's *A*-major Sonata. Instead of closing the econd period exactly like the first, the composer gives it an imperfect uthentic cadence, and appends the perfect cadence in a rhythm of wo measures.

33.

62. BEETHOVEN appends to the close of the three-part small primary form (see Fig. 31 a),

a group of seven measures, thus:

In the Rondo of the same Sonata (see Fig. 48),

he extends, in the same way as MOZART in the example cited above (Fig. 63), the close of the second period by two measures:

A similar extension is seen in the Theme of the *Largo appassionato* of the *A*-major Sonata, Op. 2:

63. Here, however, the composer leads the Antithesis of the second period into the key of the *Subdominant,* before bringing it to a close. Thereby the four measures of the Antithesis are augmented to seven.

64. The extensions thus far noticed are limited to the addition of but few measures. But in the A♭-major Sonata, Op. 26, we find in the Trio a two-part primary form whose second period is extended to *double* the length—16 instead of 8 measures—and thus belongs to the *large period-form*. Pieces like this, therefore, hold the middle place between the large and the small primary form, being made up of component parts of both forms.

NINTH EXERCISE (1).

Work over, by extension, some of the small two-part primary forms composed for the fourth exercise.

65. In the *small three-part* primary form are found extensions of the same kind. Thus, the third part in the *Allegretto* of BEETHO-VEN's *F*-major Sonata, Op. 10, is enlarged, first, by an interpolated imitation, occupying two measures:

next, the last four measures are repeated in the lower octave,

and finally, a closing-group (or period?) of 8 measures is added.

In this way the third part of this small three-part primary form is extended, by *interpolation, repetition,* and *Coda,* to *almost threefold length,* forming 22 instead of 8 measures.

66. A similar course is pursued with the middle group of the Scherzo of BEETHOVEN's *A*-major Sonata, Op. 2, No. 2, beginning thus:

This motive predominates in the first part, which is repeated.

The second part modulates, with the same motive, from *A*-major in 8 measures to *g*♯-minor, whereupon a 2-measure cadence in this key follows. But then an entirely new phrase is formed in the same key—*g*♯-minor—which leaves the key at the 8th measure, to modulate back to *A*-major in five measures.

Hereupon follows, according to the rule, the first part as **third** part, *but* with a Coda of four measures.

67. In the Rondo of the *e*-minor Sonata, Op. 90, the small three-part primary form is carried out according to rule, *but*—the *middle-group* is repeated:

while Thesis and Antithesis (see Fig. 29 c) have no repetition.

We observe, incidentally, that we have here a small three-**part** primary form, each part of which makes a perfect authentic tonic cadence, the second part, in consequence of the repetition, even *twice.*

NINTH EXERCISE (2).

Make extensions of some of the small three-part primary forms already composed as exercises.

68. Extension of the *large two-part* primary form is seen in the *Adagio* of the *G*-major Sonata, Op. 31. The close of the first period is here in the sixteenth measure, where also the Thesis of the second period begins.

This Thesis of the second period has 10 instead of 8 measures, and in the 10th has moreover a protracted cadenza

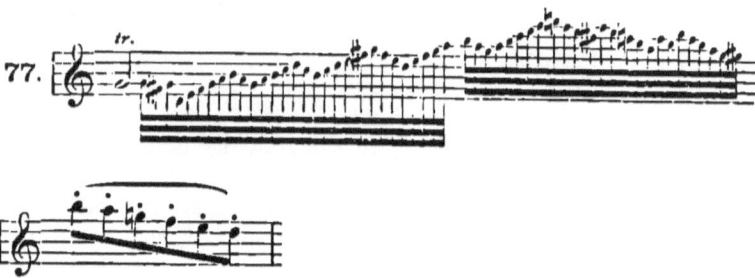

which leads back into the 8-measure Antithesis.

69. Similarly, in the Theme of the Variations with which the $A\flat$-major Sonata, Op. 26, begins, the middle-group, Thesis of the second period, is lengthened by two measures:

70. The extension may of course be applied to any part of the large two-part primary form, though further exemplification is not deemed necessary.

NINTH EXERCISE (3).

Enlarge some of the large two-part primary forms already composed.

71. Although the *large three-part* primary form is in itself of very great dimensions, yet it is very often extended to still greater ones.

Instead of many examples in abridgment we give here one in its entirety, the Scherzo of BEETHOVEN's Third Sonata. It begins with a 16-measure period, based on an imitation. The period is repeated.

79.

The second part, immediately following this, begins with the same imitation, and after sixteen measures is also found in the key of the Dominant, hence is ready to lead into the third (repeated first) part.

80.

This transition into the third part is, however, here delayed by a varying repetition of the half-cadence formula, which takes up 7 measures—the eighth measure is at the same time the first one of the third part.

To the regularly constructed third part is added a Coda of 9 (8+1) measures.

82.

NINTH EXERCISE (4).

Extend some of the pieces in large three-part primary form already composed.

CHAPTER XIII.

ABBREVIATION.

72. Abbreviation applies, of course, chiefly to the *large* primary forms of great dimensions, especially to the *three-part* form.

73. An example of abbreviation of the *first part* is found in BEETHOVEN's 1st Sonata, in the Minuet, whose first-period consists of $3 \times 4 + 2 = 14$, instead of 4×4 measures. (The second part also is here reduced to 14, the third to 12 measures.)

74. The *second* part is frequently composed, after the manner of the small primary form, of 8 measures, as for example, in the Minuet of the *D*-major Sonata, Op. 10.

Here the first part is regularly composed of 16 measures, closes in the tonic harmony and is repeated.

83.

The second part, however, has only *8 measures,* and consists of a sequence through the circle of Fourths, *b*-minor to *D*-major, in 4×2 measures:

75. In such cases, which are very frequent, large and small form appear united; as it were, mixed. (In the example quoted the subsequent third part is considerably *enlarged,* from 16 to 29 measures.)

76. In Mozart's *Eb*-major Symphony the second part of the Minuet is also reduced to 8 measures:

The third part of the same is lengthened by 4 measures.

77. In the Minuet of the great *C*-major Symphony of the same master the second part is reduced to 12 measures:

TENTH EXERCISE (1).

Compose abbreviations of large three-part primary forms.

78. In the large *two-part* primary form abbreviations are in general not advisable, as too noticeably disturbing the symmetry of the two parts, which is not the case to the same extent in the *three-part* form.

79. In the *small three-part* primary form occasionally occurs abbreviation of the middle-group, as in the next two examples:

In the *Andante* of BEETHOVEN's *D*-major Sonata, Op. 28, the last part is abbreviated by two measures.

80. The *small two-part* primary form, as being already of the smallest dimensions, rarely exhibits abbreviations.

TENTH EXERCISE (2).

Abbreviate one or two small three-part primary forms.

CHAPTER XIV.

COINCIDENCE OF THE FINAL AND INITIAL MEASURES (OVERLAPPING).

81. It often occurs, especially in larger constructions, that the last measure of a group coincides with the first one of the next group; in other words, that a group begins with the same measure with which the preceding group closes, so that one single measure combines in itself end and beginning. Such a measure is to be regarded as belonging equally to both groups, and thus counts double. This peculiarity of *overlapping,* as it is called, is indicated in rhythmical cipher by a *tie,* placed *behind* the figure for the *final* measure, *before* the figure for the *initial* measure. Thus, for instance, 4⌣ indicates a 4-measure group, or Tetrameter, whose final measure at the same initiates a new group; on the other hand, ⌣4 indicates a Tetrameter whose *initial* measure at the same time ends a group immediately preceding. In the practice of the young composer thus far, such measures occur almost exclusively in the transition from the middle-group into the last part, whether the latter form the third period or the Antithesis of the second. Thus, for example, in the middle-group quoted in

Fig. 86 (MOZART), the third part begins at the last measure; its first measure therefore coincides with the last one of the second part.

In the same way the measure

in Fig. 79 belongs in the later course of the piece both to the *third* part as *beginning* and to the *second* part as *close* of Fig. 81, and ekes out the second part into an *Octameter* (group of eight measures).

82. In counting the measures, however, it must be carefully noticed *with which metrical part the group begins*, for, in the theory of form the measures do not count *from bar to bar*, but *from one metrical part to another of the same order*,—here, for instance,

from the *second quarter-note* of each measure to the *second quarter-note* of the following measure. See Par. 3.

The student should, by way of practice, alter some of his previous exercises, introducing some few groupings of this kind, in which the initial measure and the final measure overlap.

CHAPTER XV.

IRREGULAR GROUPINGS OF MEASURES.

83. We have already seen that in the *regular* rhythmical order the measures are grouped by 2, 4, 8, 16, etc. Among the *irregular* groupings which make exceptions to the general regularity observed in the different forms, the most common are the *Trimeter* (3-measure group) and the *Pentameter* (5-measure group).

84. The *Trimeter* may be regarded as either an *extension of* the *Dimeter* (2-measure group), or a *contraction of* the *Tetrameter* (4-measure group). The Minuet of MOZART'S *g*-minor Symphony begins with two Trimeters.

These may be regarded either as extensions of the Dimeters in Fig. 93 a, or as contractions of the Tetrameters in Fig. 93 b.

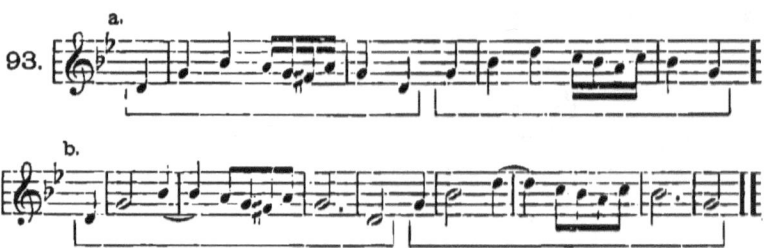

85. The special esthetic effect of such irregular formations is based on this—unconsciously made—comparison with the regular formations.

86. BEETHOVEN and his successors often expressly mark such Trimeters as *Ritmo a tre battute* (rhythm of three measures). The most notable example of this is in the Scherzo of the Ninth Symphony, where the trimeter

serves for a very extensive thematic elaboration.

87. The *Pentameter* is most generally regarded as formed from a *Tetrameter* by *extension*—the following, for example,

95.

from

or from

and the following opening of MOZART's small *D*-major Symphony,

96.

say, from

etc.

88. Other irregular groups of 7, 9, 11, 13 measures, are likewise seen to be extensions or contractions of the regular formations nearest to them.

89. The irregular groupings of measures are of importance for larger constructions, in so far as they from time to time effectively interrupt the uniformity of the two-measure rhythmical order. In general it will be found that precisely the greatest masters of form are partial to free and bold construction, and by no means like to be restricted to the limits of uniformity in rhythmical formations.*

90. Not to be confounded with the Trimeter, the Pentameter, and other organically irregular rhythms, are certain seemingly irregular groups arising from the extension of the regular form of the phrase, etc., by short additions *external to the form*, therefore not to

---

* A curious instance of rhythmical irregularity is found in one of MENDELS-SOHN's " Songs without words,"—No. 30, in *A* major (Spring-song), in which the large opening period ends at the 15th instead of the 16th measure.

be reckoned as really modifying it.   Some of these extensions shall now be noticed.

91. For making a marked separation, when desirable, between two phrases, an *additional measure* is sometimes employed instead of a *pause* over the last note of the first phrase, as in the following examples :

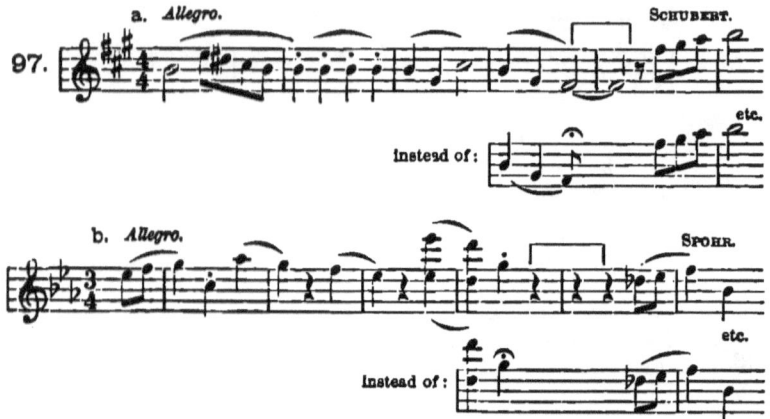

The above two phrases are to be regarded as composed each of *four measures,* the measures marked by the bracket being really external to the rhythm.

92. The addition of a measure or two over and above the rhythmical form is sometimes for the sake of *uniting* phrases or periods, etc., forming as it were a *link* between them.   This is often the case when a *new key* is to be introduced.

CHAPTER XVI.

LICENSES OF MODULATION.

93. To any one who has studied *harmony*, modulation in any form can, of course, not be difficult, and to the experienced contrapuntist it can be but child's play. Exercises in modulation can, therefore, at this advanced stage of our study, be dispensed with. In the *composer's practice*, however, the requirement of *novelty* often decides in favor of a more heterogeneous modulation, even without an evident inner necessity. It is not requisite to assign the experiential or logical limitations of such procedure, the student's *absolute mastery* over the harmonic material being assumed as a matter of course. Nevertheless, let one example show how what is *seemingly heterogeneous* results from *inner necessity*, then appears *in itself well grounded, in keeping with its context*, and *conformable to nature*.

94. In the most celebrated of all funeral marches, that in BEETHOVEN'S *A♭*-major Sonata, Op. 26, occurs the extraordinary modulation from *a♭*-minor into a close of a part in *D*-major.

The March itself belongs to the three-part primary form. It forms at first an 8-measure period, which closes in the *parallel major key*—*C♭*-major, and whose Thesis ends with a Half-cadence (on the dominant); so far all is *perfectly regular*. But now, *instead of repeating this period*,—whether literally or with some variation,—BEETHOVEN *transposes it* into the *minor mode* of the afore-mentioned parallel key—that is, into *c♭*-minor. From this transposition arises the modulation, for the parallel key of *c♭-minor* is *E♭♭-major*, which is enharmonically the same as *D-major*. Of course, BEETHOVEN introduces, for greater ease in reading, the enharmonic change already at the entrance of *c♭-minor*, which he writes as *b-minor*.

95. This transposition might be regarded *simply* as a repetition, like one indicated merely by : ‖, if BEETHOVEN, from the 6th measure on, while substantially keeping up the modulation, yet had not *carried it out differently*. For, the *first time*, he passes by way of the *dominant* key of *a♭*-minor—*e♭*-minor—into the *parallel* key—*C♭*-major; but the *second* time, by way of the *subdominant* key of *b*-minor—*e*-minor—into the parallel key, *D*-major. This difference in the manner of carrying out what is substantially one and the same modulation, militates against the conception of this case as one of mere (transposed) repetition.

96. We have here, then, a *double-period* (see Par. 36) of
(2 × 8) measures, as *first part* of the primary form.

97. The *second part* (middle group) is shortened to four measu
with transition into the *third part*. The modulation from *D*-ma
into the (major) key of the dominant of *ab*-minor—*Eb*-major, is
once effected by means of the diminished septimachord—*d*—*ab*—
cb, enharmonically substituted for *d*—*g♯*—*f♮*—*b*. See Fig. 87 b.

98. The third part has period-form and is extended to ten me
ures. There is no repetition.

99. All things being considered, we are compelled, in determ
ing the form, to decide in favor of the *small three-part primary for*
in which *duplication* has taken the place of *repetition* of the f
period, while the second part is reduced to half of the regular ext
sion, and the third, otherwise normally constructed, is enlarged
two measures.

With the *esthetic significance* of this march and of its modulat
we are at present not concerned. This is acknowledged with adm
tion by the musical world generally, so that there is scarcely anotl
composition of the same kind to be compared with it.

ELEVENTH EXERCISE (1).

Transpose this march into various keys, either in writing or at o
on the pianoforte.

100. It is not unusual to find, in modern pieces in primary fo
in the major mode, a close of the first period in the *major key of*

Mediant,—for instance, in *E*-major in a piece in *C*-major,—being a variant of the common close in the *minor* key of the Mediant (see Par. 34). Again, in a piece in *minor,* the first part sometimes closes in the *major* key of the Dominant,—in *G*-major, for instance, in a piece in *c*-minor. Generally speaking, in modern music the greatest stress is laid upon characteristic harmonization (modulation); hence the striving after singularity *in this particular direction* must be regarded as specially characteristic of the age. This circumstance calls for special practice in modulation, opportunity for which shall now be afforded.

ELEVENTH EXERCISE (2).

N. B.—In the exercises under this head, the forms of the *usual cadences* are to be *avoided.*

(a) *Compose 4-measure phrases which make an unusual modulation.* [*In the major mode a phrase often effectively closes with an authentic cadence in the key (minor) of the* SUPERTONIC.]

(b) *Compose* LARGE PHRASES *(see Chapter VII) of the same kind.*

(c) *Compose* PERIODS *of this kind with cadences of the parts in unusual keys.*

(d) *Compose periods of this kind with unusual cadences both of the parts and of the close.*

(e) *Unite such periods into pieces in primary form.*

SIXTH DIVISION.

THE MOTIVE AND ITS DEVELOPMENT.

CHAPTER XVII.

NATURE OF THE MOTIVE.

101. Every musical thought which serves as subject of a musical elaboration may be called the MOTIVE of such elaboration. The term "motive" is, however, generally applied to those smaller tone-groups out of which a musical thought is spun. In this sense the motive is generally contained within the limits of *one measure,* and is then the

last unit, or tone-group forming a whole, into which the *section* may
be resolved.

102. The doctrine that the motive is *generally* contained within
the limits of one measure must be understood as implying, first, that
the motive sometimes *exceeds* those limits; and secondly, that it does
not always *fill out* one measure. The motive forms a model for
elaboration chiefly in its character of well-defined *rhythm* (as we shall
presently see); hence the limits of the motive would seem to be those
of the *rhythm*, irrespective of the number of measures. In the application of this principle, however, there may be diversity of opinion,
without practical importance.

103. The following period

is clearly spun out of *four motives*. Measures 2, 5, 6, have the same
rhythms as 1, the model rhythm, filling out one measure. Measure 4
is tonally different from 3, but rhythmically the same. Here, too, the
motive fills out one measure, as does motive 4 also. Motive 3 fills
only *half* of the measure. Evidently, then, what makes measures 1,
2, 5, and 6, one and the same motive, despite melodic differences, is
the rhythmical similarity; and the same is to be said of measures 3
and 4, and of the two diminutive tone-figures marked "motive 3."

104. In the period given in Fig. 101 there is less clearness as to the construction and the number of the motives. If the limits of the several *rhythms* are to be regarded as those of the motives, the period is constructed from *three* motives, each contained in *two measures.* In this view, the small tone-figures severally contained in measures 1 to 6 constitute *motive-members.* These same tone-figures may, however, be regarded as severally constituting the *motives* of the period, as indicated by the shorter brackets below the staff.

105. It is clear, then, that a motive is not subject to the limitations of one measure, but may either exceed it or fall short of it, and that one and the same melody may be analyzed—reduced to motives—in various ways. The motives must, however, always be recognizable as the germs of the melody, in order to serve for thematic elaboration. As a rule, they will not exceed one measure, without being reducible to several smaller *members ;* they may on the other hand be very short, consisting of two notes, or even of one note followed perhaps by a rest. The shorter they are, the greater is the necessity that they should be rhythmically striking. As to the *number of motives* to be employed in a piece, it may be said in general that the fewer there are of them—provided they are well exploited* and are in themselves interesting—the better for the unity and intelligibility of the piece. Not many motives, but few motives, striking and thoroughly elaborated,—this has ever been the rule of the heroes of tone-poetry. There are not lacking in the compositions of the masters themes developed from a single motive, and sometimes a short one at that. The first period of BEETHOVEN'S violin and piano Sonata in *A*-major, for instance, is spun out of one single short motive (or motive-member), thus,

* A word from the French, signifying to exhaust, to work, to turn to account, to make the most of, etc. See Worcester's Dictionary (1881), Supplement.

In composing sections, phrases, and periods for his exercises, the student has thus far not been called upon to consciously spin them out from small tone-figures as germinal musical thoughts. He may now, after having become acquainted with the rudiments of formal structure, give his attention specifically to the systematic development of the motive into the section, the phrase, etc., by the various processes to be detailed in the next chapter.

CHAPTER XVIII.

DEVELOPMENT OF THE MOTIVE.

REPETITION.

106. The attentive student will have observed that in a great number of the examples thus far given in this work, a motive is developed by REPETITION, in a stricter or a looser sense. In fact, since development implies a certain similarity to the original type, each of its different processes comes under the head of a certain kind of repetition. Nevertheless, for greater clearness we shall make a separate classification of those processes which fall more strictly under this head.

107. The repetition of a motive is either *absolute* or *relative*. The former kind, of course, includes all the features of the motive—rhythmic, melodic, and harmonic, conjointly, as in the following example:

103.

108. Under *relative* repetition are included the various *transpositions* of the motive to other degrees of the scale, its principal feature—the rhythm—remaining unaltered, or not materially altered. Examples of this are Figs. 10, 14, and the following:

Sometimes this transposition involves *modulation*, for instance:

109. The repetition, *in a certain regular order*, of a figure composing a motive constitutes what is called a SEQUENCE, which is of a
rythmic, or a melodic, or a harmonic nature, or of all three combined.
Here follows an example in which all these three natures are united.

In the above example, the figure marked ⌐ a ⌐ is immediately
repeated twice, the same melodic and harmonic progression being
transposed each time *one degree higher*. Such Sequences most gener-
ly occur enriched with ornamentation, figuration, etc., as in the
following example, which shows how BEETHOVEN treats the above
sequence in the last repetition:

BEETHOVEN.

107.

110. As a rule, repetition in sequence-form should be used w great moderation, as excess in this point induces monotony a betrays poverty of ideas.

TWELFTH EXERCISE (1).

(a) *Point out, in such instrumental works as BEETHOVEN MOZART'S, and HAYDN'S Sonatas, Symphonies, etc., developments motives by the various methods of REPETITION just explained.*

(b) *Develop many ORIGINAL motives into sections and phrases applying to them the same methods of repetition.*

ALTERATION OF INTERVALS.

111. Another means of the elaboration of a motive is to chan one or more of its *tonal relationships, i. e., intervals,* substituting larger denomination for a smaller one, and vice-versa, a smaller fo larger one. In the former case, as when, for instance, a motive repeated with the change of the original *Second* into a *Third, Four* etc., or *Fourth* into a *Fifth, Sixth,* etc., as the case may be, we ha what we may call INTERVAL-EXPANSION. The following examples:

BEETHOVEN.

a. *Prestissimo.*

108.

b. *Maestoso.*   HAYDN.   c. *Andante.*   HAYDN.

112. INTERVAL-CONTRACTION is, of course, precisely the opposite of expansion, as illustrated in the following examples:

TWELFTH EXERCISE (2).

(a) *Point out in the works previously mentioned developments of motives by interval-expansion and contraction.*

(b) *Develop many original motives into sections and phrases by the same means.*

RHYTHMIC DIMINUTION AND AUGMENTATION.

113. When the notes of a tone-figure or a rhythm, considered as a motive, are represented by *smaller values* than the original ones, and thus the number of measures is reduced, we have what is called RHYTHMIC DIMINUTION, as in the following examples:

114. The opposite of diminution is AUGMENTATION, which is
much more frequently used for developing motives than the former,
although both occur oftener in the contrapuntal than in the free style.
Here follow examples of rhythmic augmentation in the free style.

REMARK—That not *all* the notes of a tone-figure or a rhythm are necessarily
included in augmentation (and the same is to be said of diminution also), is evident from the first two of the above examples, at **d** and **e**, where the notes have
the same value as in the original.

TWELFTH EXERCISE (3).

*Develop motives—new, or already composed for previous exercises—
into sections and phrases by rhythmical diminution and augmentation.*

CHAPTER XIX.

DEVELOPMENT OF THE MOTIVE (Continued).

INVERSION.

115. INVERSION is applied to a motive when the tone-figures and rhythms are set in *contrary motion.* Here a careful distinction must be made between notes of *equal* and those of *unequal value,* and between *accented* and *unaccented* metrical parts and members.

116. In the following examples of simple tone-figures of notes of *equal value,*

measures **aa, bb, cc, dd.** show the *inversion* of **a, b, c, d,** respectively. It will be noticed that by the inversion the notes are for the most part differently accented, the original *primary* accent (marked ∧) being exchanged for *non-accent* (⌣), the *secondary* (') also for non-accent (except in $\frac{3}{4}$ meter, as at **bb**), and vice-versa, the non-accent for either the primary or the secondary accent.

The following examples illustrate inversion of this kind (in the last two the tone-figures are inverted in the Octave):

Also the passage-like place in BEETHOVEN's Sonata, Op. 26,

is, from the second half of the sixth measure on, repeated i
inversion:

117. In cases of tone-figures composed of notes of *unequal* valu
an *exact inversion,* both rhythmic and tonal, would give results lil
the following:

Here the rhythmic motive, as such, is changed, and (especially
bb and **cc**) entirely distorted. And even though figures like the
inversions are under certain circumstances admissible, yet they reser
ble the original motives so little as to seem rather to be new ones. I
therefore, the original motive is to be recognizable in the inversio
this can be effected only by the retention of the characteristic *rhyth*
unaltered, applying the principle of inversion to the *tones* only, as
the following examples, in which the inversions—marked **aa, bb, c
dd**—should be respectively compared with the inversions similar
marked in Fig. 116.

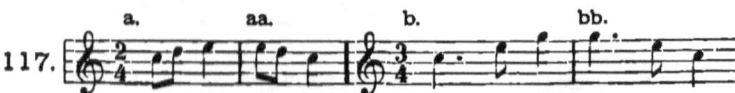

Here follow illustrations of rhythms inverted in this manner:

118. The exact—at once rhythmical and tonal—inversion of tone-figures as motives, exemplified in Fig. 116, is called RETROGRADE INVERSION, as distinct from the kind last illustrated, which is simply inversion, in a restricted sense.

119. Rhythms comprising many measures and heterogeneous tone-figures should be constructed with special care, if they are, on the one hand, to serve as motives for retrograde inversion, and, on the other hand, to be connected, when thus inverted, with their respective

original motives, and form phrases having a musical sense.   The
lowing two examples show, each at **b**, the exact retrograde invers
of the corresponding four-measure rhythm at **a**:

THIRTEENTH EXERCISE.

*Compose sections, phrases, and periods, by the inversion of moti
in both the ways just explained.*

CONTRAPUNTAL TREATMENT.

120. An additional means of developing a motive is CONTI
PUNTAL TREATMENT.   Thus, for example, the motive of BEETHOVE:
$B\flat$-major Sonata, Op. 106,

is worked up, in the development-group, into a kind of free canon :

So, too, in the *c*-minor Symphony of the same master, the principal subject of the last movement (Allegro),

is worked up in canonical imitation, thus:

CHAPTER XX.

DEVELOPMENT OF THE MOTIVE (Concluded).

VARIATION.

121. Tone-figures and rhythms are often developed by VARIA-TION, the usual way being to represent notes of greater value by figures of two or more notes, yet so that the original motive may be recognizable. The variation may be restricted to single parts (members) of the motive,—as represented by the bracket in the following example :

or, it may extend to the entire motive, examples of which may be found in any "Theme with Variations." In pieces in larger instrumental form also are sometimes found variations of this kind, as, for example :

122. The dividing a metrical part into its members—which we may call ARTICULATION—inducing tone-multiplication, and the opposite process of reducing the number of tones by *contracting* metrical parts or occasionally omitting one, also come under the head of Variation. Here follow examples of each:

(In the above figure the bracket indicates the articulation of the corresponding notes on the upper staff.)

(The bracket in the above figure marks the omission of the anacrusis with which the first of these two dimeters begins.)

FOURTEENTH EXERCISE (1).

Develop motives by means of VARIATION, etc.

DISMEMBERMENT AND ENLARGEMENT.

123. Larger motives may be *dismembered, i. e.*, reduced to *smaller ones* by detaching from the original rhythm one or more tone-figures, or notes, belonging to it. These detached tone-figures serve as motive-members for further developing a melody. They are taken indifferently from either the beginning or the end of the original motive.

124. By an opposite procedure, *shorter* motives may be *combined* with other motives to form *larger* ones. Thus (to illustrate this latter procedure first), the 1st movement of BEETHOVEN's Seventh Symphony is based on this short principal motive, ♩♪ | ♩ ˙ , which appears in manifold combinations, as, for instance,

So too, in the same master's c-minor Symphony (No. 5), the shor motive ♪♪♪ | ♩ |, which predominates throughout the entire fir movement, appears in the following enlarged form, among others:

125. The reduction of larger motives to smaller ones is illustrate in the following examples:

In the same way, in BEETHOVEN's c-minor Symphony, 1st movemen from the motive enlarged from the principal motive (see Fig. 13(above) two half-notes are detached, and serve for development throug several measures:

132.

Moreover, the small tone-figure , occurring in the same movement, is merely a reduction of the already short chief motive

In the Sonata, Op. 106, BEETHOVEN uses for development the
principal theme,

133.

in the abridged form of only three tones,

134.

afterwards the first *two* tones alone appear:

135.

The first part of the Minuet of HAYDN's *B*-flat Symphony (No.
5), is developed from the first two measures:

136.

HAYDN dismembers this rhythm into the following motives:

and combines these fragments into an organic whole.

Many more examples might be cited, showing how the disintegration of a rhythm or tone-figure may furnish ample material for the elaboration of musical thoughts.

FOURTEENTH EXERCISE (2).

(a) *Dismember larger motives into smaller ones.*

(b) *Combine detached motives with other motives to form larger ones.*

THE PASSAGE.

126. A final means of development is the PASSAGE, which is a rapid tone-series, passing by degrees or by skip through optional intervals, ascending or descending, and for the most part repeating a determinate figure. Thus, in BEETHOVEN's *G*-major Sonata, Op. 31, which begins as follows:

the motive in the second measure is afterwards worked up into the following Passage:

BEETHOVEN.

In the above, the first measure (formed by transposition from the 2d measure in Fig. 138) is the rhythmic and melodic model for the second measure, which latter has thus the character of *sequence* (see Par. 109).   The third measure is the literal repetition of the first, the fourth that of the second, each an Octave lower, so that the same correlation of model and sequence is kept up; and the same is to be said of the fifth and sixth measures respectively.   In the seventh measure the motive-member is *inverted*, with partial *interval-contraction*.   In the eighth measure—first half—is the transposition of the first half of the seventh measure; the second half is a transposition, with *interval-expansion*, of the first half.   The ninth measure is the transposition an Octave higher of the seventh measure.   The tenth measure, finally, introduces a new tone-figure, extended by transposition and inversion through five measures, whereupon a point of rest, but no Cadence, ensues.   This whole passage accordingly belongs to none of the fixed rhythmical forms hitherto described.

BEETHOVEN's Sonata in *f*-minor, Op. 57, affords an additional example of a passage, formed on the motive inclosed in a bracket, in the following figure:

140.

127. The frequent introduction of the Passage is not to be reco
mended, as inducing monotony and betraying poverty of ideas.

FOURTEENTH EXERCISE (3).

Develop tone-figures into passages, after the above models.

SECOND PART.

APPLICATIONS OF THE PRIMARY FORM.*

FIRST DIVISION.

COMPOSITE PRIMARY FORMS.

CHAPTER XXI.

THE THEME WITH VARIATIONS.—THE STUDY (ETUDE).

128. Groupings of musical thoughts in primary form, constituting independent pieces of music or independent portions of larger pieces, give rise to the COMPOSITE PRIMARY FORMS. These rule almost without exception the boundless domain of *dance-music* proper (*i. e.*, composed for actual dancing), and of the higher and lower orders of *parlor-music* and *pastime-music*. In the Symphony, the Scherzo (Minuet, Episode, Intermezzo) belongs almost always to these forms, which are frequently met with also in other domains of composition.

129. The simplest form of combination of independent musical thoughts is found in the THEME WITH VARIATIONS. Here the same thought is first presented in simple form, then repeated in different variations, which, while retaining the same harmonic basis, develop various figural motives, contrapuntal imitations, etc., sometimes also change the mode, or even the key. The Theme has generally primary form, sometimes period-form.

BEETHOVEN's creations in this form, and those of other masters, old and new, are well known. The last movement of the *Sinfonia*

---

* In all the following exercises the student should, when it is practicable, make use of his former exercises.

Eroica belongs to this form, which also is predominant in the last movement of the *Ninth Symphony.* The extreme limits of the form are indicated by BACH's "*Air with 30 Variations,*" BEETHOVEN's *Variations on a Waltz by* DIABELLI, and his *32 Variations on a theme in c-minor.* As a specially popular, charming, and noteworthy work of this class, the *Andante in C-major,*

of HAYDN's *G*-major symphony may be mentioned.

How BEETHOVEN has constructed out of the period given in Fig. 32, a theme in primary form, and composed variations on it, may be seen in the KREUTZER *Sonata,* Op. 47.

The Variations in RAFF's *g*-minor *Suite* for Piano may be classed as models ; so also, in the sense of the noblest virtuosity, LISZT's Variations in the *Don Giovanni Fantasia* on the celebrated theme,

130. The ETUDE or STUDY is *in a certain sense* a variation *without theme ; i. e.,* its basis is the general scheme of a primary form, rather than a particular theme. It consists essentially of the manifold variation of a motive designed for technical practice. The more connected it appears in this respect, and the more strictly the *unity* of the piece is hereby maintained, the greater the freedom in which it can indulge in the structure of its groups and in modulation.

131. Many Etudes exceed the limits of the primary form, as, for example, CHOPIN's charming *e-minor Etude,*

which has a Trio with an entirely different chief motive.

144.

In this and similar Etudes technic is subordinated to the esthetical principle of delivery, which in the case before us requires a contrast to the airy lightness of the first part, and finds it in the *Trio*.

132. Just as there are many studies which, in no wise intended for technical practice, are (like the above-quoted and many others by CHOPIN and others) wrought into charming pieces of music; so, too, many a piece of music receives the name of Etude without having been originally written for the purpose of the Etude, merely because it has technically adopted its form, and the modesty of its author conceals its higher aim.

CHAPTER XXII.

THE DANCE-FORMS PROPER.

133. The chief forms of the SOCIETY–DANCE are based upon a *2-measure step,* which involves a complete rotation and at the same time a motion forwards of the body. Each *single* measure serves for only a half-rotation of the body. After *two measures,* therefore, the dancer begins again with the same foot. Hence it is *altogether unallowable* to introduce in one of these dances phrases or periods with an *uneven number of measures,* as, trimeters, pentameters, heptameters, etc. Even such groups of 6 or 12 measures as are not strictly based on *two-part division,* may easily cause disturbance in dancing. The periods should therefore, as a rule, be limited to 4, 8, 16 measures. Occasionally, however, the most prominent composers of this kind of music indulge, by way of exception, in 10, 12, 20, 24-measure periods and similar constructions.

134. The usual form of the POLKA is the following:

(1) Short *Introduction* in Polka-tempo, mostly 2 or 4 measures.

This does not form part of the dance, and therefore need not | regularly constructed.

(2) *Polka.* Large two-part primary form, each part repeated thus, 2 × ‖: 16 :‖.

(3) *Trio.* Similarly constructed, often introduced by a short merely rhythmical prelude of two or four measures, as,

This little prelude does not interrupt the dance.

(4) *Repetition of the Polka* with *Coda* (Appendix), which gene ally embraces 8 measures or somewhat more, and shows evident sigr of a close. The Coda *is not part of the dance.*

135. The rhythm of the Polka is based on the combination of th following 1-measure motives:

$$\frac{2}{4}$$

Upon these the melody is built up.*

In the *piano-forte Polka* the left hand keeps up the rhythm of th dance, playing the bass and the chord following it, or sounding with (as above illustrated), while the right hand sustains the melody. Th *orchestration* of dance-music belongs to the theory of instrumentation

136. Most analogous to the *Polka* is the common MILITAR MARCH, which, however, is written in alla-breve meter, $\mathbf{C}$, has there fore quarter-notes instead of the eighths of the polka-rhythm.

137. The GALOP has the same form as the Polka, but is a *quic* $\frac{2}{4}$ meter, with *but one beat* to the measure; thus, 1 | 1 | 1 |, etc whereas the polka has 1—2 | 1—2 |, etc. The Galop is often con posed in large *three-part* primary form.

138. The POLKA MAZURKA is a slow $\frac{3}{4}$ meter, which likes t accentuate piquantly the weak metrical parts, and is partial also t dotted rhythms. Its principal form is:

(1) *Introduction :* few measures in the Mazurka *tempo.*

(2) *Mazurka.* Large three-part primary form; first part, secon

---

* At concert-performances dances are *rhythmically shaded, i. e.,* the temp is frequently changed, sometimes in the most arbitrary manner. To this the ind cations of change of *tempo* refer in the scores of some dance-composers.

part, repetition of the first part, each time 16 measures *without* repetitions.

(3) *Trio.* Large three-part primary form; also with abbreviated (8-measure) second part.

(4) *Repetition of the Mazurka,* and short *Coda.*

139. The *Trio,* in almost all of these dances, is in a key *other than that of the principal movement,* mostly in that of the *Subdominant. Minor keys* are only exceptionally admissible for actual dances, as, for instance, for the purpose of humoristic treatment; here they should be entirely omitted.

140. The most peculiar and prominent form of the society-dance proper is the WALTZ. This is a quick $\frac{3}{4}$ meter, in which each measure has but one beat. The form of the Waltz is entirely different from that of the other dances. Its composition requires, in a higher degree than that of the other dance-forms, a special talent for the melodies of the dance. Its *most usual* form is the following:

(1) *Introduction,* mostly consisting of matter entirely foreign to the dance, often *Adagio,* Fantasia with prominent parts for solo-instruments, leads to the

(2) Short *" Entrance"* in the waltz-tempo, 4 measures, leading directly into the

(3) *Waltz.* 5 numbers, counted No. 1—5 (*sometimes* only 4, *seldom* only 3).

These 5 numbers, which constitute the *Waltz proper,* may be of similar or dissimilar structure. They consist, however, *almost always* (for our present exercises *always*) of two 16-measure periods, each of which is repeated. If they have *three-part* form, the third part is merely the repetition of the first.

Nevertheless these periods are mostly so constructed as *not to thematically correspond* one with another within one number, thus constituting two periods in conjunction without any further connection. The same applies to the closes, which indeed seldom modulate far from the principal key, yet are not strictly bound to the Tonic. The key of the separate numbers is of course independent.

(4) *Finale,* instead of the short Coda an elaborate Finale in waltz-tempo, repeating the most successful numbers of the Waltz, often (Potpourri) introducing a new one.

141. It is to be observed, moreover, that *rhythmical variety* finds the widest range in the waltz-melody, and that whilst the bass and middle voices constantly sustain the dance-rhythm, the melody soars above it with the most *unrestrained freedom.*

142. *Harmonic* effects are, however, here as in all dances to be applied very sparingly, as they too easily distract the attention from the proper aim of dance-music.

Examples are so numerous that it is not necessary to call attention here to special ones.

FIFTEENTH EXERCISE.

Compose, in the principal forms just described, dances, especially Waltzes.

Compose to the following basses various dances, after transposing the basses into another key and indicating the proper meter by its signature.

THREE-PART PRIMARY FORM.

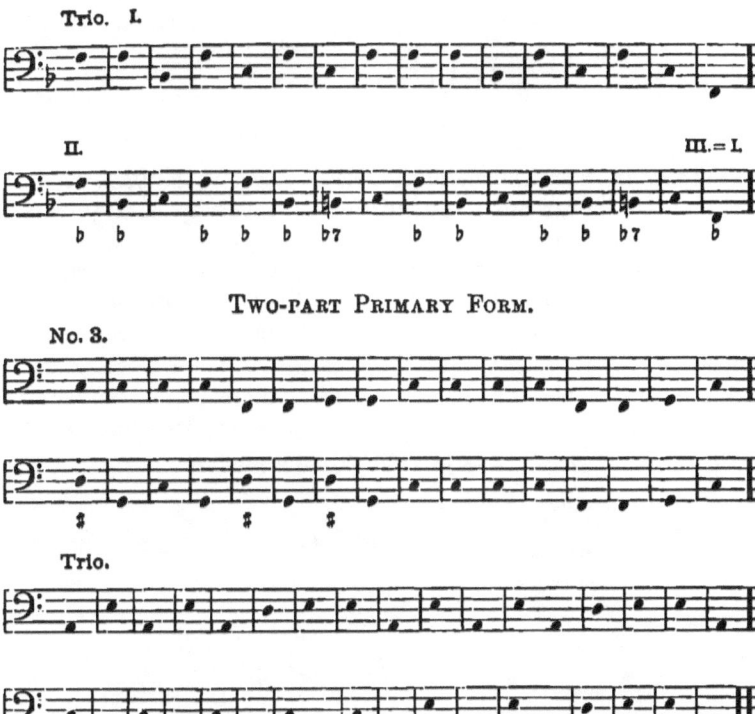

The determinate arrangement of the measures—whether, for example, the initial measure shall be *complete* or *incomplete*, etc., as also of course the rhythm, which here constitutes the proper subject-matter of the exercise, are left to the judgment of the composer. It is also free to him to replace at pleasure the *fundamental basses* here given by the corresponding *derivative* basses, or to substitute for them other basses from the works of favorite composers.

CHAPTER XXIII.

THE MARCH-FORMS.

143. In the MARCH, and the related forms of the POLONAISE the QUADRILLE, there is no rotation of the body, consequently two-measure step proper.

We have already spoken of the MILITARY MARCH in connec with the *Polka;* it is in a certain sense the lowest form of the ma:

144. The FESTIVAL MARCH is in $\frac{4}{4}$ meter. To every meas there are two measured steps of the marchers, but four or two b of the baton. That the measures should be grouped in *even* num is *not unconditionally necessary* here. The celebrated March in M ERBEER'S " *Prophète* " begins even with a *pentameter.*

146.

145. The March, No. 22, in *" Le Nozze di Figaro,"* exhibits original construction in the evidently *intentional* monotony of group-closes, which are nearly all in *G.* In the very first five me ures of the melody *G* predominates, the first 8-measure group cle in *G*-major, hereupon follows a group of two trimeters, both of wh also close in *G.* The first part thus embraces 14 measures, and is peated. The second part corresponds on the whole to the first, thesis again closes in *G,* the antithesis, in the same kind of hexame (double trimeter) as at the close of the first part, turns to the To Hereupon follows a Coda of 4 measures, forming a short close in tones of the tonic harmony.

This March, which in the opera has only scenic significance, yet actually serves for marching, has no *Trio*.

146. The Festival March is not restricted to determinate rhythmical figures, like the dances, but must, of course, make the measured step distinctly prominent. Its most usual form is the small two-part primary form for March and Trio. *Prelude* (often in the form of a Fanfare), Entrance to the *Trio*, and *Coda*, according to circumstances.

147. We add here the construction of two of the most celebrated and admired march-compositions of modern times, which have already served and will still serve as models for many others : MENDELSSOHN's "*Wedding March*" in the "Midsummernight's Dream," and WAGNER's "*Tannhäuser*" March, both of which properly come under consideration here, as they serve for actual marching (on the stage).

148. Both compositions begin with an introductory trumpet-fanfare :

MENDELSSOHN.

148.

In MENDELSSOHN'S March this Introduction leads at once into th
Theme, which is based on the celebrated harmonic progression:

WAGNER'S Introduction, which by its transition to the Dominai
has the character of a Thesis, does not lead directly into the them
but is repeated, interrupted by allusions to later motives of the Marc]
three times—only at the third time leading into the theme, with ɛ
interpolated transitional passage:

WAGNER'S Introduction accordingly shows 23⌣ measures again
4 in that of MENDELSSOHN.

149. MENDELSSOHN constructs his *Theme* in small three-pa
primary form:

First Part: 2 × 4 = 8, repeated, = 16 measures.
Second Part:
Thesis: 8
Antithesis: 2 × 4 = 8

together 16, repeated, = 32 measures

together 48 measures.

But MENDELSSOHN includes in the repetition of the first peric
the 4-measure Introduction, whereby the first part amounts to ;
measures.

So far, then, the length of the whole, including the Introduction itself, amounts to 56 measures.

From here on MENDELSSOHN'S March is kept more within the limits of the composite primary forms already discussed, whilst WAGNER'S March approaches in construction the large symphonic instrumental forms to be considered later.

MENDELSSOHN, that is to say, now introduces a *Trio* in *G*-major:

leading to a repetition of the principal theme, which is this time abbreviated to an 8-measure period.

Then follows a second *Trio* in *F*-major:

after which the whole Theme without repetition, with rhythmical movement by means of figuration:

the Introduction with increased sonority:

lastly, a brilliant *Coda* of 2 × 8 + 10 ⌢ measures.

In all the parts, except the first, the composer avoids dences. This gives to the March that character of constant forward, with the esthetic effect of *suspense*, which WEBER among the older masters, so well knew how to attain in his

150. WAGNER constructs his Theme not in primary fo a large 16-measure period:

and immediately joins to it another theme in the same key, likewise in 16-measure period form:

158.

Here the *Thesis* makes a *Half-cadence* on the *Dominant septima-chord:*

159.

the *Antithesis* an *authentic* cadence in the *key of the Dominant,* modulating into it:

160.

Another 16-measure division now follows, showing, however, t
form not so much of a period as of a double-phrase, since the *seco:*
part (which takes the place of the Antithesis) ends with a Ha
cadence.   In the bold modulation of this phrase this Half-cadence
made in *C♯*-major.

We have now already three 16-measure periods, the first formin
tonic period, the second a period which modulates into the Domina
the third consisting of two corresponding phrases, which, start
from the Tonic, modulate, the first into the Dominant, the seco
into the key situated a major Fifth above this Dominant.

Now again begins a new division—of which there are foreshad
ings in the Introduction—begins, in fact, immediately with the *mi
Subdominant* of the key in whose *Dominant* the preceding divis
closed:

162.

The harmony with which this division begins is to be taken as
Tonic f♯-minor. The Thesis closes with an imperfect authentic cadence in *F♯-major,* and just as the *G♯-major* Triad above was followed
by the minor Triad on *f♯,* so here the major Triad on *F♯* is followed
by the minor Triad on *e.*

163. etc.

The Antithesis now passes in the fifth measure to the Dominant
of the principal key, whereupon the introductory trumpet-fanfare is
again heard ; thus this Antithesis embraces 12 measures = 4 + 8.

*Now begins with the principal theme the repetition of all that has
been had,* with accompaniment of the Chorus.

To this entire repetition, comprising 68 measures, is again joined
the principal theme in *fortissimo* and with enlivened rhythm by means
of figuration.

164. *ff*

The *Coda,* which brings the March to an end, thematically exhausts
the first and the second theme and the Introduction.

In LISZT's piano-arrangement of this celebrated March, the tender
theme which in the opera accompanies the entrance of the minstrels,

165.

forms the *Trio proper* of the March.   It is, however, not a part of t[]
March in the *original*, which we follow.   We regard WAGNER's Marc[]
in fact, as a March with many parts (independent themes) but *witho[]
Trio.*

151. The two Marches here considered have this in common th[]
the beginning of the principal theme forms a *complete cadence* (thus[]
closing formula).*   The principal theme of MENDELSSOHN's Marc[]
in particular, must be considered strikingly bold and original, t[]
ginning, as it does, with harmonics foreign to the key.†

152. We will now place side by side the respective schemes[]
both Marches:

---

* In MENDELSSOHN's March:

In WAGNER's March:

In each of the above cadences the Supertonic Triad may be regarded as supplyi[]
the place of the Subdominant Triad.

† An example of a Festival March opening, like MENDELSSOHN's Weddi[]
March, with harmonics foreign to the key, though not forming a complete *Cade[]*
is LISZT's "Huldigungs-Marsch," in *C*-major.   This March opens abruptly on []
Dominant septimachord of the key of *F*, and that, too, in what we may call []
boldest form, *i. e.*, with the Seventh—*Bb*—in the Bass, which then makes the b[]
progression to *F*, instead of the usual resolution to the degree below.

MENDELSSOHN, *Wedding-March.*

Measures.

Introduction, 4 measures.

Principal Theme: Small three-part primary form with repetitions.......... 16

FIRST TRIO, IN *G*-MAJOR.

First Part: extended phrase-form, Thesis—Half-cadence on the Dominant, 6 measures, repeated.... 12

Second Part: Double-phrase, *B*-major—*G*-major, imperfect authentic cadence, 2 × 4 measures, repeated..... 16

Repetition of principal theme shortened to a period, without repetition....... 8

SECOND TRIO, IN *F*-MAJOR.

First Part: Phrase-form, 8 measures................... 8

Second Part: Phrase-form, 8 measures, repeated......................... 16

Transitional Group: Thesis—*d*-minor, Half-cadence on Dominant, 8 measures; Antithesis transitional, 8 measures................ 16

Repetition of principal theme: Small three-part primary form, 3 × 8........ 24

Coda: Introduction, 4 measures; thematic reminiscence, 8 measures—repeated, 16 measures; close, 10 measures............................. 30

Total, 182

WAGNER, *Tannhäuser-March.*

Measures.

Introduction: Entrance, 4; Middle-group, ⌣4⌣; Entrance, 4; Mid.-gr., ⌣2; Mid.-gr. (fourth theme), 4; Mid.-gr., 2⌣; Entrance, 4; Mid.-gr., 4⌣. 23⌣

Principal Theme: Tonic Period.............................. 16

Second Theme: Modulatory Period..................................... 16

Third Theme: Double-Thesis.. 16

Fourth Theme: Double-phrase with transition (8 + 4) + 8 measures....... 20

Repetition of all four Themes... 68

Repetition of principal Theme: Thesis as above; Antithesis with delayed close.. 17

Coda, 8 measures, beginning on the *B*-major Triad in $\frac{6}{4}$ form; second theme; 8⌣; Entrance and close, 21............................. 36

Total, 212

153. The FUNERAL MARCH has the slowest *Largo* as *tempo.* BEETHOVEN has, in a pianoforte Sonata, furnished the unapproachable model of it. (See Fig. 99). CHOPIN's Funeral March—only second to BEETHOVEN's in popularity—is also found in a piano-forte Sonata. The Funeral March is—with few exceptions (among them HANDEL's Dead-March in "Saul," in *C*-major)—in *minor*, the *Trio* almost always in *major*, viz: in the *parallel* major key, in the major key of the *same Tonic*, or in that of *the major Third below* (**Submediant**).

154. The construction of BEETHOVEN's Funeral March in *ab*-minor has already been given (Chapter XVI.). The Trio, in *Ab*-major, consists of two 4-measure phrases, which are repeated. The repetition of the March is followed by a *Coda*, closing in major.

155. The POLONAISE is a lively March in $\frac{3}{4}$ meter, with a step to every quarter-note. The characteristic figure of the Polonaise is this:

It is not necessary, however, that this figure should be invariably adopted and carried out, as is proved by many examples. It is also characteristic of the Polonaise, that in most cases the last two measures of its periods are rhythmically divisible into three measures of $\frac{2}{4}$ meter, as, for example:

168.

WEBER.

156. The QUADRILLE (CONTREDANSE) is likewise related to the March, but is written in $\frac{2}{4}$ and $\frac{6}{8}$ meter, and has *two* steps to each measure. It has six divisions, separated one from the other by pauses; the last passes immediately into a dance proper (round dance).

SIXTEENTH EXERCISE.

Compose Marches and Polonaises, especially in the principal forms which have been given.

CHAPTER XXIV.

IDEALIZED DANCE-FORMS.

157. There are countless compositions which, without being intended for dancing or suitable for it, borrow from a given dance-form, mostly in great freedom, the *rhythmical motive* and the *most general characteristics of construction.* No form has been more productive in this respect than the *Waltz,* whose idealizations by SCHUBERT, WEBER ("Invitation à la valse"), but especially CHOPIN, are everywhere celebrated. These charming creations combine all the elegancies of an art-technic developed to the utmost with the dance-rhythm employed with the most perfect freedom. Through CHOPIN and many others, who are for the most part his imitators, the form also of the *Mazurka* and the *Polonaise* has experienced such an ideal development. Other national dances too, such as the *Bolero,* the *Tarantella,* etc., have been treated in this manner. Of late years, prominent composers have shown a similar interest in the *obsolete dance-forms* of past centuries, the *Saraband, Gavotte, Bourrée,* etc., etc. Especially noteworthy are RAFF's labors in this field.

158. Our classical composers have devoted special attention in this sense to the *March.* BEETHOVEN's Funeral March in the "Eroica" symphony, that in the $A\flat$-sonata, of which mention has already been made, the Festival March in the *A*-major Sonata, Op. 101—

Vivace alla marcia.

169.

with the canonical Trio, the March in the " Ruins of Athens," etc
may be assumed as well-known. MOZART's " Alla Turca " from th
A-major Sonata—

170.

is likewise an example in point. A peculiarity of this piece is th
8-measure period which follows each part as a kind of Coda.

171.

In CHOPIN's Funeral March in $b\flat$-minor the left hand has an impressive imitation of the ringing of bells, a kind of " Basso ostinato," found also in the 2d Impromptu and an Etude of the same master.

159. But the most important among the *idealized dance-forms* is the form which has sprung from the obsolete *Minuet,* and which under the name MINUET or SCHERZO has found an abiding place in the large instrumental works of our classics.

The form of this movement is mostly large two-part or three-part primary form, variously modified by means of augmentations and abbreviations now of this part, now of that, as has been illustrated by many examples in the first part of this work. The Trio is only exceptionally in the key of the Dominant, mostly in the same key, and in minor movements, in the *major* key of the *same tonic.* In MOZART's $E\flat$-major and C-major symphonies the Trio remains in the same key; in the g-minor symphony in the major key of the same tonic. In HAYDN's D-major symphony (No. 1) the Trio is in the key of the *Submediant of the minor key with the same tonic,* viz: in $B\flat$-major, a not unusual relationship of the parts in point of modulation. In BEETHOVEN's 1st, 2d, Eroica, 4th, Pastoral, and 8th symphonies the Trio is, like that of MOZART's symphonies above alluded to, in the same key as the Scherzo; in the 5th (c-minor) and the 9th, in the major key of the same tonic; in the 7th, in the *major key* of the *Submediant, i. e.,* in D-major, the Scherzo being in F-major. The 7th symphony is the only one of BEETHOVEN's in which the Scherzo is *not* in the same key as the symphony.

160. HAYDN's symphonies and quartets—not only the favorite ones but also those numerous ones that are less known—afford an inexhaustible assortment of consummate models of that species which approaches more nearly to the original form. Such are to be found also in MOZART's instrumental works, in countless pianoforte-sonatas, duos, trios, string-quartets by BEETHOVEN. Of the symphonies of the last-named master the Scherzos of the 1st, 2d, 4th and 8th are kept within the same limits. We must here call attention to the manner in which BEETHOVEN developed this form in other works, how he enlarged and transformed it in the Scherzo, by some examples calculated to incite the beginner in composition to a more profound study of the others also.

161. In the 7th—A-major—symphony the first part of the Scherzo exhibits singularity of formal structure in the 2-measure introduction alone,

172.

which thenceforth constantly serves as connecting-link of the parts.
It is interesting, from the standpoint of modulation, that the close of
the first part is made in *A-major* (key of the symphony), this key
being in fact reached by a sudden transition from *F*-major, by means
of the chord of the augmented Sixth.

173.

The first part, as a whole, consists of a 16-measure *period of the
fourth form* (Par. 27), whose antithesis is lengthened by a cadence-
formula of six measures, while the period itself is preceded by a
2-measure Introduction.

On the other hand, the *second part* so far exceeds the usual limits
of our form as almost to assume the character of a development (as in
the Sonata-form). After four measures of the introduction-motive
(Fig. 172), the repetition of the motive—

174.

(compare Fig. 173)—partly of the whole of it, partly of its 2d measure
only, gives rise to an 8-measure group, whose second motive, transposed to *D*-major,

175.

is repeated four times, whereupon it appears in *c-minor*—

176.

etc.

and leads, after three measures, into the dominant harmony of *C*-major. Thus, then, we have—excluding the Introduction—a composite group of $8 + 4 + 4 = 16$ measures, modulating from *A*-major to *C*-major. This group is now repeated in exactly the same way, *but*—this time modulating from *C-major* to *B♭-major*. A similar repetition in *B♭*-major now seems about to take place, but already in the third measure the introduction-motive is added to it,—

177.

Oboe and Bassoon in 8ve.

Violins and Viola.

etc.

and leads to the entrance of the first 8-measure group, with repetition, which the Bass then takes up, followed by the other voices in *imitation* (the last voice in contrary motion), leading into the third part (repetition of the first).

178.

crescendo.

Beginning.

f

etc.

The close is made first in *C*-major with closing formula of 8 measures,
then with the same formula extended to 12 measures, in *F-major*.
After this perfect close the introduction-motive finally holds on (for
4 measures) to its upper note, *a*.   During this *a*, which enters *tutti ff*,
and remains *p* in the violins, the *Trio* in *D-major* begins, is regularly
carried through in enlarged three-part primary form, with a 14-meas-
ure Coda, closing with the noted progression of the dominant septima
chord of *D*-major to that of *F*-major:

This chord leads back to the Scherzo, which is repeated entire, excepting only the repetition of the second part.

Hereupon re-entrance of the Trio with all repetitions and Coda.

Second re-appearance of the Scherzo, this time *without* repetitions.
The Coda again sustains for four measures the *a* which introduces the
Trio.   But only the first two measures appear, the first in *major*, the
second in *minor*, then short close of five measures, *presto*.

162. Still more peculiar is the construction of the Scherzo of the 5th (*c*-minor) symphony. The Thesis—

181.

is repeated with a slight extension. A new theme then enters:

182.

which, beginning in *c*-minor, makes a half-cadence in *E♭*-major, is then repeated in *c♭*-minor with half-cadence in *G♭*-major; in *four measures* more it reaches the Dominant harmony of *e♭*-minor and here constructs a half-cadence formula of 8 measures. The Dominant of *e♭*-minor, viz: *B♭*-major, now serves as starting-point for the repetition of all that has preceded, this time from *b♭*-minor to *C*-major as Dominant of *f*-minor, instead of from *c*-minor to *B♭*-major as Domi-

nant of *cb-minor*. The repetition of the first thesis is this
extended from 8 to 18 measures, and employed for modulating
c-minor.

The Dominant of *f-minor*, viz: *C*-major, now becomes again
tonic *c-minor*. The first theme is repeated, the second half of
repeated in passage-form;

hereupon a *counterpoint* against the principal motive of the them
the Bass, is made by a charming flowing melody in the upper v
which forms a perfect cadence,—

his cadence being further strengthened by an 8-measure Coda. With
he exception of these two cadences the whole movement exhibits
alf-cadences.

The *Trio* is carried through with less irregularity; it is technically
otable for its *fugal* elaboration,—

nd the strong bass-figure with which the second part begins. The
rst part closes regularly in *G*-major, the second in *C*-major. At the
epetition of the latter, however, it changes the *cresc. al ff* of the first
ime into a *diminuendo al pp*, and leads, without a close, immediately
nto the repetition of the Scherzo. The inspection of the continuation
f this fine movement is left to the student, who should follow up the
ints we have given for this kind of score-study.

SEVENTEENTH EXERCISE.

*Compose Minuets and Scherzos, but without intentionally exceeding
he limits of the primary form.*

CHAPTER XXV.

SPECIAL FORMS.

163. There is also a large number of characteristic and import
compositions—among them many of the most original creation
which, without adhering to any special dance-form, belong to the
mary forms which we have thus far described. In the first rank
here to be mentioned those compositions of these forms in *slow ten*
which, under the name of "Elegy," "Ballad," "Song without Wor
or under various other titles, partly of a descriptive character
"Melancholy," "Resignation," "Nocturne," "Berceuse," etc., f
independent pieces of music, or appear as parts of larger compositi
To the latter kind belongs, for instance, the *Andante* of BEETHOV.
Sonata, Op. 28, whose separate parts have already been illustrated
Figs. 42, 88).

EIGHTEENTH EXERCISE (1).

Compose a slow movement in composite primary form.

[Models for the separate parts are found in abundance in the first part of
work.]

164. The number of compositions of the kind we are conside:
in *quick tempo* is no less great. An unusually attractive exampl
this kind, CHOPIN's "Impromptu," Op. 29, shall here be analyzed
being specially instructive.

The left hand carries through a figural motive which is interes
on account of the inserted changing-note *d*♮,

187.

which, however, we can only notice in passing, as we wish to call
student's attention to the *construction* exclusively.

The entire composition is carried through in uninterrupted mot
The closes are for the most part veiled by lively figuration.

The *first part* (which is based on the motive cited above) has *three-part* primary form of 8, 10 and 16 measures.

The *Trio* has *two-part* primary form of 16 and ‖:16:‖ measures.

The *repetition* of the first part is note for note, a short *Coda* leads to the close.

If we now turn our attention to the separate parts, we find at the beginning a regular period of the second form, consisting of Thesis and Antithesis, each of 4 measures:

188.

The second part modulates to and fro, from $E\flat$-major to $b\flat$-minor, back to $A\flat$-major, between $A\flat$-major and $E\flat$-major:

189.

hereupon follows a chromatic succession of sextachords,*

190.

---

* Sextachord, a shorter expression for "Chord of the Sixth."

the repetition of which adds two measures to the length of this pa
which then, with a half cadence, passes into the repetition—the thi
part.

The comparatively great extension of this third part is no long
new to us, but for a better inspection of the extensions it will be a
vantageous once to represent the group without them, as in our fi
exercises, and to reduce it to the measure of the first period.

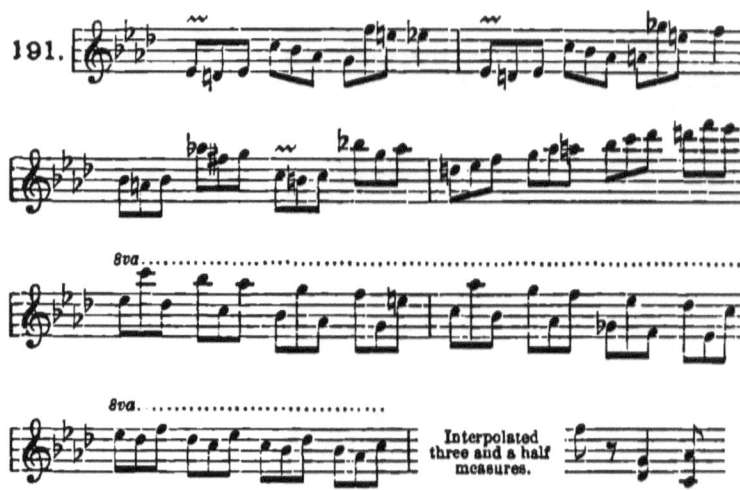

191.

Here follow the Coda and the transition into the Trio.   T
interesting modulation in the Trio is left to the observation of t
student.   It remains only to remark, that the second period of tl
two-part primary form has no immediate thematic relationship wi
the first.   Similar combinations are of frequent occurrence in MOZAR'
works, especially in his operas.

EIGHTEENTH EXERCISE (2).

*Compose a piece of music in composite primary form, in qui
TEMPO, and independent of any special dance-form.*

[The chief point here is to avoid a stereotyped, dance-like rhythmical form
accompaniment.]

SECOND DIVISION.

THE LOWER RONDO-FORMS.

CHAPTER XXVI.

THE RONDO-FORM, IN GENERAL.

165. The lower RONDO-FORMS also are essentially based on certain independent elementary forms, yet they are distinguished from the composite primary forms by a more direct—closer—connection of the parts. At the same time they often come in so close contact with the primary form that it is difficult to tell one from the other. For—as on the one hand the primary forms occasionally relax the strictness of their boundary-lines,—the Rondo-form, on the other hand, sometimes admits a more rigorous limitation.

166. The peculiarity of the Rondo-form, to which it owes its name * (Round-song, or Circle-song), is the *digression* from a chief subject and the *return* to it. But the *special feature* by which the Rondo is most essentially distinguished from the composite primary form—especially as the latter is exhibited in the dance-forms,—consists in the *metrical and rhythmical freedom of both construction and tonality.* Here rhythmical uniformity entirely disappears. The fantasy, left to itself, enjoys perfect freedom of construction and rhythmical conformation, but, at the same time, *has one support less.*

167. The Rondo-forms are divided into the *lower* and the *higher.*† The lower are based on the primary-form and its elements exclusively, the higher partly on the SONATA-FORM, acquaintance with which they accordingly presuppose.

168. Among themselves, the lower Rondo-forms are distinguished

* From the "Rondeau" of the French poetry, in which the first strophe, after being followed by a second, is repeated. The old English "Roundelay" was somewhat similar in form.

† Sometimes the terms "large" and "small" are used instead. They are not, however, to be recommended in this connection, as they apply to the *extent* of the Rondo, which is not necessarily involved in the distinction with which we are at present concerned.

one from another by the *number of the themes* employed.   The follow
ing distinctions are made :*

Rondo of the first form, with *one* theme :
Rondo of the second form, with *two* themes :
Rondo of the third form, with *three* themes.

CHAPTER XXVII.

RONDO OF THE FIRST FORM.

169. In the Rondo of the FIRST FORM there is but *one* independen
theme.   Between this and its repetitions there is no construction o
any complete form, such as the primary form, the period, and th
large independent phrase (see Chapter VII.).   Other forms of th
phrase are not regarded as sufficiently complete to constitute a them
over against the chief theme.

The *theme* has always a clearly defined form, mostly primary, o
that of a large *period,* seldom that of a large, extended phrase.

The *episodes* of this form are either *thematic, i. e.,* working u
some thought of the chief theme, or, *of a character entirely their ow*
i. e., introducing *new motives,* but not working them up into any con
plete form.

The *repetitions* of the theme are as a rule *varied.*   This is the ca
particularly in slow *tempo,* which is specially peculiar to this form.

The *close* is often enriched by a *Coda* (mostly thematic).

170. An example of such a Rondo is afforded by the *Largo appa.*
sionato of BEETHOVEN'S *A*-major Sonata, Op. 2, whose theme h
extended two-part primary form (see Figs. 68, 69).   After the close o
the theme the following phrase begins in *b*-minor,

---

* A writer in GROVE'S "Dictionary of Music and Musicians" says, speakir
of the gradual development of these three forms : "The Rondo-form was th
earliest and most frequent definite mould for musical construction. * * * * *
Starting with a principal subject of definite form and length, the first idea naturall
was to preserve this unchanged in key or form throughout the piece.   Hence
decided melody of eight or sixteen bars (measures) was chosen, ending with a fu
close in the Tonic.   After a rambling excursion through several keys, and with 1
particular object, the principal subject was regained and an agreeable sense o
contrast attained.   Later on there grew out of the free section a second subject i
a related key, and still later a third, which allowed the second to be repeated i
the Tonic. * * * * * * The first of these classes is the Rondo from COUPERIN 1
HAYDN, the second and third that of MOZART and BEETHOVEN."

192.

which in the 4th measure makes a complete close in $f\sharp$-minor. It is immediately repeated in this key, the melody being given to the middle voice,

193.

then, with a new motive—

194.

betakes itself to the Subdominant of the principal key, and thus returns to the theme, which is repeated, note for note, without variation. To this is joined a group of four measures, connecting with the middle-group of the theme, with the following imitation,—

195.

which is repeated in heightened figuration:

196.

At the last measure of this group the theme begins in *mi*
with a powerful harmonic climax to the dominant, where
appears, shortened to an 8-measure period, with new figure
second voice,

197.

and the whole movement closes with a Coda of 8 measures.

NINETEENTH EXERCISE.

Compose a Rondo of the first form in slow tempo.

171. Of all applications of this form the *Andante* of Br
c-minor Symphony may perhaps be regarded as the most
the most perfect model. Though it is taken for grant

student of composition is perfectly familiar with this movement, yet it must here be subjected to a technical analysis, not only to serve as a model of formal structure, but also to call attention to the finished manner in which the *variations* of the theme are here introduced and worked out.

The *theme*, which is given in Fig. 50, is enlarged, by a group developed out of the close, from *eight* to *twenty-two* measures. To this is joined—rhythmically connecting with the first figure of the theme —a group of 27 measures, beginning in *A♭*-major:

198.

afterwards, with the remarkable transition from *pp* to *ff*,

199.

making a cadence in *C*-major. The same group then begins, this time given to the brass-instruments, in *C*-major,

200.

and modulates thence in *pp* back to *A♭*-major, when the first variation is introduced :

201.

This variation, with somewhat enhanced figuration, is applied t
all that has preceded.

The second variation, which now follows—

202.

is limited to the chief subject proper (8 measures), is repeated climac
terically, and leads directly into the *third variation*:

203.

This closes in the tenth measure on the dominant, and here begins
developing itself out of the motive

204.

the four-voiced phrase for flute, oboe and clarinet, which finally lead
back into the place in *C*-major (Fig. 200) with increased tone-volume
From this a figural modulation leads to the last two variations, th
first of which is *minor*.

205.

whilst the second takes on a free *canon* form:

206.

The subsequent *più moto* and *a tempo* is a closing Coda.

172. In *quick tempo* the first Rondo-form is best modelled on the enlarged three-part primary form, from this launching out into passages, runs, modulations, etc., then repeating the chief subject in abridgment, again digressing from it, and closing with a more complete repetition of it, with Coda. Example, BEETHOVEN's Sonata, Op. 10, No. 3, *Rondo Allegro*.

REMARK.—It has already been pointed out that the *Rondo* and the *composite* primary form are very easily confounded. But the extended *simple* primary form may also be confounded with the Rondo-form. An extremely clear illustration of this is the *Andante un poco adagio* of MOZART's Sonata in *C*-major:

207. etc.

This long piece of music, numbering 79 measures—

Andante un poco adagio.

208. etc.

is nothing more than an extension, by means of written out an varied repetitions of the several parts, of a *two-part* (or two to thre part) primary form in the following proportions:

First Part:	Thesis....................................	8 measure
	Antithesis..................................	8 "
	Varied repetition...........................	16 "
Second Part :	Thesis...................................	12 "
	Antithesis.................................	8 "
	Varied repetition...........................	20 "
	Lengthening of the close...	4⌣ "
	Coda.....................................	4 "
		79 "

CHAPTER XXVIII.

THE RONDO OF THE SECOND FORM.

173. In the Rondo of the SECOND FORM *two* themes stand ov against each other, of which the second has most generally about tl same relation to the *key* as the Trio in the composite primary forn has to the principal theme, *i. e.*, it is only exceptionally in the key the *Dominant*, mostly in the *parallel* key, the homonymic* key. *Maggiore* (major) against *Minore* (minor), and vice-versa,—in the k of the *Mediant*, or occasionally in a more remote key.

The *first* theme is constructed like the theme of the first Rond form.

The *second* theme is either introduced by a modulation, or connec immediately with the first. In the latter case it very closely approach the composite primary form, yet with this difference, that here tl structure of the theme is not necessarily in that form.

On the other hand the second theme shows a decided tendency lead back, *before forming a close*, into the first theme.

174. Whether the alternation of the two themes takes place on once or several times, is, as far as concerns the determination of tl

---

* That is, having the *same name* (Tonic), but differing in *mode*. Thus, tl scale or key of *C*-major and that of *c*-minor are homonymic scales or keys. On tl other hand, two scales or keys with *different names*, though they may be of tl same *mode*, are *heteronymic*, as for example, *C*-major and *e*-minor, or, *C*-major ai *A*-major, etc., etc.

form, immaterial; as also, whether the themes are repeated entire, or with abbreviation, or with extension.

175. The most brilliant model for this form, although closely resembling the composite primary form, with principal subject and Trio, is the incomparable *Allegretto* of BEETHOVEN'S *A*-major Symphony.

The short subject (see Fig. 44 b) in two-part primary form, on which this great composition is based, and which by repetition of the last 8 measures is extended to 24 measures, is first repeated in three variations, beginning with the combination of violas, violoncelli and basses, and leading up to the display of the full power of the orchestra. A short transition—

then leads into the second theme, which is in *A*-major, and sustains in the bass the rhythmical motive running through the whole piece.

The second theme has the following structure:

Period (with Thesis as above, Fig. 210) closes in *E*-major
    (Dominant) .... 16 measures.
Interpolated imitation-group, as in the following fig., 3 × 2 =   6   "

Period of 2 × 8 measures, closing the first time in the principal key, the second time in *C*-major...............	13 meas:
The above imitation-group in *C*-major.................	6 "
Total number of measures in second theme,	44 "

There is no return to the beginning; the movement breaks here, and passes into the major dominant harmony of *a*-minor.

Hereupon follows the *fourth variation*, in which the flute, oboe bassoon have the counterpoint (Fig. 45), the bass the theme, the vic and viola the figuration. This variation is lengthened by a C Immediately upon this follows a *fugato* on the theme—

as *fifth variation*; it ends with a figuration for wood wind-ins ments in *ff*, against the principal motive carried by the string quar trumpets, horns and kettle-drums, in 8 measures, with a decisive c in *a*-minor.

Hereupon the transition given in Fig. 209, slightly varied, repetition of the second theme—abbreviated to a period closing to ally, with a Coda of 4⌣ measures.

Short movement of 8 + 4 measures, from the chief subject.

Last variation, and close.

The subject in A-major cannot be considered as a variation of principal theme, for lack of the harmonic conditions; nor has it independence of construction necessary to a *Trio*. We may there rightly regard it as *second theme of a Rondo of the second form*, wl *principal theme* has many variations.

176. Of simpler construction, and more easily understood by beginner, are the Rondos of the second form in BEETHOVEN's piano-sonatas:

C-major, op. 2, *Adagio*, I, E-major, II, e-minor.
E-major, op. 14, *Finale*, I, E-major, II, G-major.
G-major, op. 31, *Adagio*, I, C-major, II, A♭-major.

besides which many other compositions of our masters might be mentioned.

TWENTIETH EXERCISE.

Compose a Rondo of the second form, TEMPO ALLEGRETTO.

CHAPTER XXIX.

THE RONDO OF THE THIRD FORM.

177. In the Rondo of the *third form* the distribution of the three themes is according to the following scheme:

> *First theme.*
> *Second theme.*
> *First theme* (abbreviated ?).
> *Third theme.*
> *First theme* (entire, or less abbreviated).
> *Coda and Close.*

The first theme has most usually (especially in quick *tempo*) extended primary form; so that the difference between the Rondo of the third form and the composite primary form with two Trios often consists (apart from the greater freedom and copiousness of the former) only in the prevalence of the tendency to transitional groups and in the abbreviation of the repetitions of the theme,—and even these differences afford no certain criterion.

178. In many obsolete, but, for all that, not uninteresting compositions of the first period of form-development in the preceding century, this form-relationship is very plainly apparent. Among these are many youthful works of MOZART, which certainly have at least an historical and biographical interest, as for example, the Rondo of the small E♭ Sonata:

The *first theme* of the Rondo here cited has large
mary form.   It is immediately followed by a subject in
in *c*-minor:

which closes its first period, according to rule, in th
The continuation—beginning of the second part, two
form—

215.

makes, four measures after, a sudden close in *c*-minor, to modulate back to the Dominant of the principal key. Hereupon follows the first theme, abbreviated to period-form.

The third theme now begins, in *eb*-minor (it is given entire in Fig. 57)—

216.

in three-part period-form of 25⌣ measures. On the final measure the first theme again enters.

This example is here purposely chosen, on account not so much of its merits as a composition, as of the simplicity and perspicuity of its formal structure. So, too, in the Rondo of the *C*-major Sonatina:

217.

and in that of the *e*-minor Sonatina (cited in Fig. 49 a), whose themes will be given later. As a transition to the BEETHOVENIAN models we will take the better-known *a*-minor Rondo of MOZART:

218.

179. The most brilliant BEETHOVENIAN example of the th
Rondo-form is the *Finale* of the Grand Sonata in *G*-major, Op. 53.
The first theme:

has extended *small* three-part primary form.   Coda and transition

Second theme, in *a*-minor:

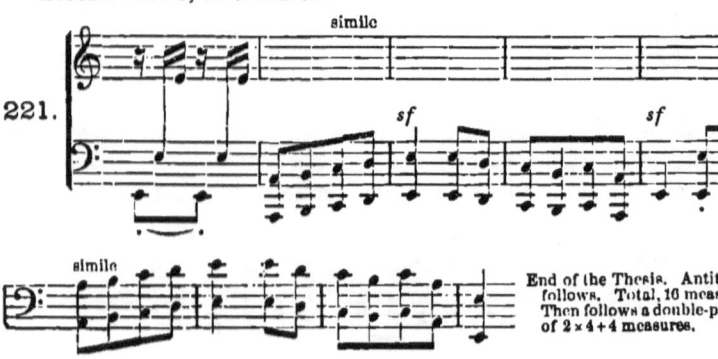

Repetition of the first theme in its entire extent.

Third theme, in *c*-minor:

(The right hand has subsequent sixteenths).

Repeated, melody in the right hand, bass *contrapuntalizes* in 16th-Triplets. Antithesis: right hand has the counterpoint (double counterpoint at the Octave).

Repeated in the inversion at the Octave, whereupon the close is repeated, once entire, twice half, and an additional close formula is appended.

First theme and close. The last repetition of the first theme is preceded by an amply developed introduction, whose starting-point is the principal motive, and which presupposes virtuosity in the executant. The repetition itself, on the other hand, is abbreviated. This is followed by a copious development of the transition-motive given in Fig. 220, and by a *prestissimo*, which is concerned almost exclusively with the first motive of the theme, and also presupposes a virtuoso.

TWENTY-FIRST EXERCISE.

Compose, according to the instructions and examples given, a Rondo of the third form in quick TEMPO.

CHAPTER XXX.

TRANSITIONAL FORMS.

180. Between the first and second Rondo-form there are TRAN
TIONAL FORMS, which seem to share the characteristics of both. Th
owe their origin to the circumstance that the middle-groups of t
first Rondo-form take an unusually independent form, or, that t
second theme of the second Rondo-form proves unusually short,
significant or vacillating.

In such cases the determination of the form is doubtful, and
have a *Rondo of the first quasi second form*, or, of the *second qu
first*.

All forms show such transitional phases, the exhaustive discussi
of which, however, would be out of place here.

181. An example of a composition vacillating between the fi
and the second Rondo-form is the *Andante* of BEETHOVEN's *E♭-ma
Sonata, Op. 7. It forms a very extended principal subject
C-major—

224.

in three-part primary form. The subject which immediately follo
in *A♭*-major—

225.

forms at first a four-measure phrase—tetrameter—closing in t
Tonic. Hereupon follows a similarly constructed tetrameter

f-minor, having the same thematic subject-matter. It begins again in *Db*-major, but modulates in the fourth measure, by means of the chord of the augmented Sixth, into the Dominant of *C*-major.

In view of the *consistent formal structure*, we might consider this as a *second theme*, and decide in favor of the *second Rondo-form*. But in view of the vacillating *modulation* the character of *theme* may be disputed, and a Rondo of the *first* form be assumed. It is, in fact, a Rondo of the *second quasi first form*.

THIRD DIVISION.

CHAPTER XXXI.

THE VOCAL SONG.*

182. In the VOCAL SONG the musical form is not *free*, in the sense of being subject to *musical conditions exclusively*, but is dependent on the poetical form and the logical laws of the language. There is good reason to believe that originally the *lyric poem* and the music to it were *one* in invention and execution; *i. e.*, that the poem was at once musically conceived. Gradually, especially through the popularization of writing, afterwards of printing, the two elements of the song were separated. Poetry became to that extent enriched with ideas, music so energetically created for itself independent forms, that both could no longer originate together, but had to be *joined*, in order to re-establish the primeval *unity* of the song—for, *song* means *sung poem*.

It is only in our time, in the domain of the grand opera, that, by

---

* The German word " Lied " is here, as usually, translated "Song ;" it is, however, difficult to define clearly and tersely precisely what that word expresses. Its character is most generally *lyric ;* yet the same name is given to a vocal composition of a *dramatic* character, such as SCHUBERT's " Erl-king," SCHUMANN's "Two Grenadiers," etc. The term is, in fact, a comprehensive one, and includes the Ballad, the National Air, the Couplet, the Comic Song, etc., also compositions for two or more voices. Among the most famous of modern composers, SCHUBERT, SCHUMANN, LISZT, R. FRANZ, and MENDELSSOHN, are especially to be named as having left noble models of this art-form, the study of which is the best possible method of acquiring the art of writing beautiful songs.

means of harmony, ripened into a perfect means of expression, union with dramatic action and declamation, a re-establishment the original state of things on a higher plane has been made possil unusually comprehensive mental gifts being of course presupposed.

There can be no question but that every musical form may imitated in poetry, thus that it is possible to adapt to a compositi kept within the limits of vocal setting, a suitable poetical text. Th is, however, something that concerns the musical *poet*, not the poeti *musician*.

For the latter the task here is the opposite one,—to compose music to a strophic poem.

The doctrine of Form is only incidentally concerned with t subject ; nevertheless, the principal points of the technical treatm of the song shall here be briefly presented.

183. The composition faithfully *follows the meter and the vers cation* of the poem, conforming them, as a rule, to the *two-meas metrical system* of music, *i. e.*, organizing them into groups of t four, eight, and so on, measures, as in the following examples:

226.

The clouds are fly - ing, the oak - woods roar,

The maid - en sit - teth up - on....... the shore;

The huge waves are break - ing with might, with migh

She sends forth her sighs.. to the dark - some nigh

SCHUBERT.

Her eyes.. all be - dimm'd are with weep - ing.

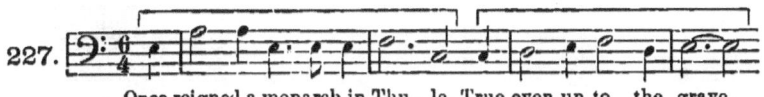

227.

Once reigned a monarch in Thu - le, True even un-to the grave,

ZELTER.

To whom his mistress, dy - ing, A gold-en beak-er gave......

(The last measure is an extension, taking the place, as it were, of a *pause*.)

228. a.

While mer - ri - ly once rid - - - ing through

cool and shad - y wood.............. ...

(By the prolongation, twice, of the emphatic tone *b* in the above, the first section seems to have three measures, the second one four; yet each section consists essentially of *two* measures, as if written thus:

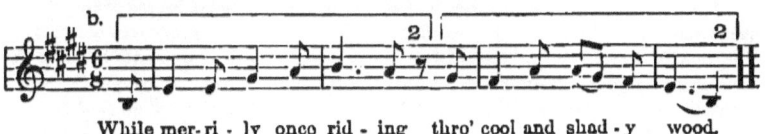

b.

While mer- ri - ly once rid - ing thro' cool and shad - y wood.

184. Occasionally the structure of the words, and other circumstances, will require grouping of the measures by *odd* numbers, at least in part of the song, as in the following example:

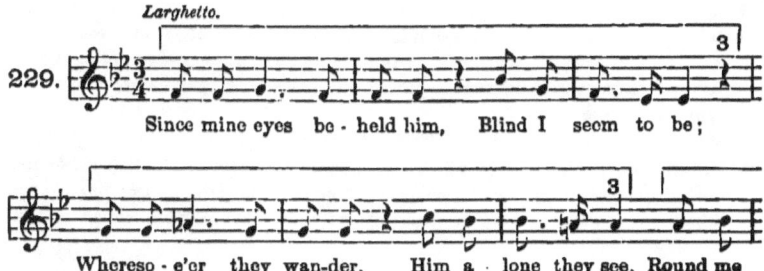

Larghetto.

229.

Since mine eyes be - held him, Blind I seem to be;

Whereso - e'er they wan - der, Him a - lone they see. Round me

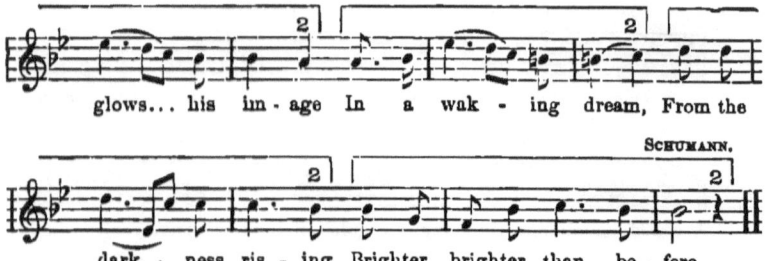

glows... his im-age In a wak - ing dream, From the

SCHUMANN.

dark - ness ris - ing, Brighter, brighter than be - fore.

185. *Repetitions of the text* may be employed, as a means of enlarging the composition and giving it greater freedom of form.
Examples of this are so numerous that quotation is unnecessary. Of
course, every such repetition of words should be *justified by their
import,* and the truly cultured song-composer will not—even for the
sake of improving the musical form—bring in a repetition which is
senseless or even absurd.*

186. The composer is bound by the inviolable law of the *logical
declamation of the text,* but in other respects, treats the text with
perfect freedom, according to purely musical laws. In the languages
of the Teutonic family the *pronunciation-accent* forms an essential
element of the *logical* accent,† which is not so strictly the case in the

---

* An instance of absurd repetition is found in a very weak sacred song, perhaps
still popular, in which occur the words: "Solomon in all his glory was not arrayed
like one of these" (*i. e.,* lilies). The meaning of this is plain enough. Yet the
composer—to judge from his repetition of the words "was not arrayed"—would
seem to have understood the meaning to be, that Solomon wore no clothes, thus
resembling the lilies of the field. "* * * * * was not arrayed—was not arrayed—
like one of these." The senseless frequent repetitions of a few words so copiously
illustrated in most of HANDEL's songs, for instance, are happily out of date, to
gether with the mannerism to which they are owing.

† The "special functions" of these two kinds of accent, says my lamented
friend the late Mr. SIDNEY LANIER in his "Science of English Verse," Chapter
IV, are:

To call the ear's attention to particular sounds in a series of syllabic sounds con
stituting an English word, for the purpose of emphasizing the special dignity
above other sounds in that word, of the *root-sound* (generally) thus distin
guished by the

PRONUNCIATION ACCENT.

To call the ear's attention to particular words in a series of English words con
stituting a sentence, for the purpose of emphasizing the logical importance
above other words in that sentence, of the word whose main sound is thus
distinguished by the

LOGICAL ACCENT.

Romanic languages (notably in the French). Faults against the pronunciation-accent are naturally less frequent than violations of the logical accent. Of these latter even the great HANDEL was not seldom guilty, as in the following examples from his "Messiah"—

230.

He shall feed his flock, etc.

He was de-spis-ed, etc.

in which the logically unimportant words "shall" and "was" receive an undue accent. So too in the air (in the same Oratorio), "Behold and see," at the words: "if there be any sorrow like unto his sorrow:" here the composer should emphasize the word "his," instead of which he sets the word twice without any accent, thus:

231.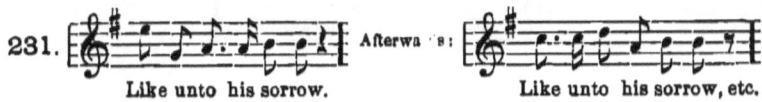

Like unto his sorrow.   Afterwards: Like unto his sorrow, etc.

187. Intimately connected with this subject is that of *Inflexion.* To borrow the language of Mr. E. PROUT:* "Just as, in speaking, we not only accent certain words, but raise the voice in uttering them, so in vocal music, especially in that depicting emotion, the rising and falling of the melody should correspond as far as possible to the rising and falling of the voice in the correct and intelligent reading of the text." In fact, the most conscientious composers make use of certain musical inflexions either corresponding to *interrogation,* or, in general, of a *declamatory* character.† Here is an example, from WAGNER'S "Lohengrin" (Act II, Scene V), of a common type of *interrogatory* inflection:

---

* In GROVE'S "Dictionary of Music and Musicians," Article, "Accent."

† "The tone-colors which arise in (expressive and poetic) speech, and the characteristic and pathetic accents which come to the front in words and syllables, constitute, at least in a low degree, a *symbolism* of its expression, and afford to music the proximate starting-points for associating itself with speech, in order to truthfully heighten that expression."—H. KÜSTER, *Populäre Vorträge,* etc.

232.

Doth doubt per-mit thee no re-pose?

Wilt thou, my name I should dis-close?

which is surely more characteristic than would be—for the same words—a *close on the tonic*, or even a *perfect cadence* in the key of the *dominant*.—In the same opera, "Lohengrin," where Elsa avows her faith in the champion who is to come to her defence, in the words—

> Des Ritters will ich wahren,
> Er soll mein Streiter sein,

which may be roughly translated thus:

> I'll bide the brave knight's coming,
> He shall my champion be;

the logical importance of the word "He" in this connection is brought out by the *declamatory inflexion* which the composer employs for this purpose:

233.

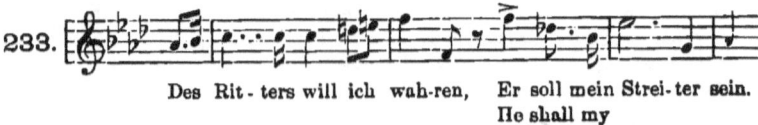

Des Rit-ters will ich wah-ren,   Er soll mein Strei-ter sein.
He shall my

and afterwards, with still greater emphasis:

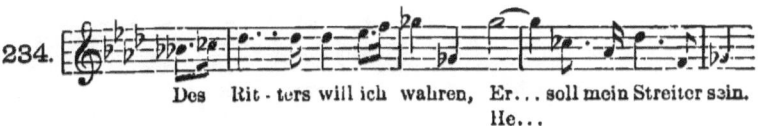

234.

Des Rit - ters will ich wahren, Er... soll mein Streiter sein.
He...

188. In the case of a song with many stanzas or (which means very much the same thing) strophes,* it is of course at the option of the composer to set *each strophe differently.* The song is then said to be *composed throughout* (after the German expression "durchcomponirt"). But when *one and the same setting* (occasional slight variations not being reckoned) is used for the whole song, the latter is said to be composed *strophically* (one strophe giving the melody for all the others). This latter mode of setting would, however, not be appropriate for songs of an epic or dramatic character, with many strophes, of which many Ballads † and Romances afford instances,—such songs should be composed throughout. Among other models of this kind of composition are SCHUBERT'S "Erl-king," and SCHUMANN'S "The Two Grenadiers."

189. It sometimes happens that in a poem for music a thought begins at the *end of a line* and runs over into the next line, as in the following couplet, translated from EICHENDORFF for a foreign edition of SCHUMANN'S "Liederkreis" (Song-cycle), Op. 39.

> Men's guile and fraud are great ; in twain
> My heart is rent with grief and pain.

Such anomalies are in general objectionable from a musical point of view, as requiring in the musical setting an exceptional adjustment of the melody,—at least the composer is bound to see that his musical phraseology does not make nonsense of the words, as, for instance :

> Men's guile and fraud are great in twain,
> My heart is rent, etc.

In the present case the English adaptation involves precisely this nonsense (the *composer* is of course not responsible, for in the German original the first line ends with a complete thought, and the music agrees with it) :

---

* Either of these words should be used instead of the expression "verse," which properly means a *line* of poetry. In this sense we speak of "blank verse."

† The *German* type of Ballad is here meant, embracing poems of a narrative character (as Bürger's "Lenore," etc.), rather than the English ballad of the present time, which is often purely lyric.

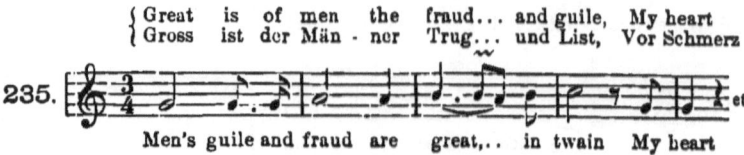

235.

In a case like the above a good *reader* would pause after "great," and closely connect "in twain" with the line following. A similar course for every similar case should be followed in the musical setting; thus in the present case, the first musical thought should end with the word "great," and a second one begin with "in twain my heart," etc. So that if SCHUMANN had had only these English words to set to the above musical thought, he would probably have constructed the latter somewhat like this:

236.

THIRD PART.

THE SONATA-FORM.

CHAPTER XXXII.

SONATA AND SONATA-FORM.

190. By SONATA is meant a piece of music consisting of several independent movements, and composed for one or two solo instruments. The number of these movements is three or four, fewer being very exceptional. On the other hand, the expression SONATA-FORM * denotes that particular form of *one movement* with which we are at present concerned.

191. The peculiarity of the Sonata-form, as contrasted with the primary form and the Rondo-form, in which the different subjects are as it were merely placed in juxtaposition, is the organic *unity* of the whole movement. If, therefore, a complete cadence is made at the end of the first division, it is in a key which is not only different from the principal key, but (for the most part) points to it, and is in close relation to it.

Hence, the intimate union of all the parts into a *whole*, which will make itself felt as such,—this is the problem to be worked out with all the means of form-structure which we have thus far acquired. In this endeavor the whole movement takes on as it were the form of a thesis farther and farther spun out; thus the need of an *antithesis* is felt, and interest is aroused. Here there is danger of going too far,

---

* SCHNYDER VON WARTENSEE uses, instead, the expression "Principal form" (Hauptform), which is a better name, seeing that the application of this form is by no means limited to the Sonata. The name "Allegro-form," proposed by some theorists, seems objectionable, as this form is not necessarily associated with a particular *tempo*.

of being too lavish with the means of climax, of losing the artistic presence of mind, which is the condition of intelligibility. The means of avoiding this danger are the clearly-marked division of the form into sub-sections, or GROUPS, the systematic modulation, the use of such cadences as will not stop the flow, being rhythmically or tonally apportioned to places which cannot serve for a complete close.

192. The Sonata-form is the usual form of the first (*Allegro*-movement of the *Sonata, Quartet, Symphony,* and kindred species of instrumental music,—also that of most *Finales* (last movements) of these species, as of *Overtures,* lastly of numerous compositions in slow *tempo.*

193. According to the *dimensions* a distinction is made of SONATINA (small Sonata-form), SONATA, and GRAND SONATA.

We shall follow up this chief form of instrumental music from the child-like simplicity of a *Sonatina* by KUHLAU to the magnificent structure of a BEETHOVENIAN Symphony-movement.

A. THE SONATINA.

CHAPTER XXXIII.

FIRST PART OF THE SONATINA-FORM.

194. The first part of the Sonatina-form is reducible to five intimately connected divisions or groups, varying in dimensions:

(1) Principal subject, or First Theme.
(2) Intermediate Group, or Link-episode.*
(3) Secondary Subject, or Second Theme (sometimes called Song-group).
(4) Closing Group.
(5) Coda.

---

* This group, as leading into a *new key* for the Second Theme, is sometimes called the "Modulation-group." Seeing, however, that it modulates *in the first part only,* and not in the *third* part, this designation is evidently not appropriate throughout the whole of the first movement of the Sonata-form except in this limited sense only.

195. These five divisions may be reduced to *two* larger ones, constituting *duality*, viz:

(1) First Theme with Intermediate Group,
(2) Second Theme with Closing Group and Coda,

by reason of the almost equal dimensions of the two divisions, the modulation which at the second theme introduces a new key and retains it, and the importance of the two themes, which constitute the essential contrast of the form.

196. If we class the *Link-episode* with the first theme, to which it is thematically most nearly related, and the *Coda* with the Closing-group, to which it is likewise thematically most akin, we have *three* divisions—*triality*, of which the Second Theme forms the *middle* one.

197. Just so naturally the *four-fold* division—*quaternity*—results from the *two* divisions constituted above (Par. 195), if we separate the first one into *First Theme* and *Link-episode*, the second into *Second Theme* and *Closing-Group with Coda*.

198. The FIRST PART of the Sonatina comes to a *perfect close,* and so far appears independent,—*but* closes in a *different key from the original one*, and *so far* appears, on the other hand, incomplete, as it were a larger thesis awaiting its antithesis.

The *key* in which the first part closes, is

in *major*, that of the *Dominant*;
in *minor*, the *parallel major* key.

The first part of the Sonatina is generally *repeated*, this repetition being sometimes introduced by a *connecting link* attached to the *Coda* and leading into the original key and the beginning.

199. Here follows, in illustration, the first part of a piano-forte Sonata by KUHLAU, written for the instruction of children, exemplifying this form within the smallest limits:

1. PRINCIPAL SUBJECT (First Theme).
Allegro.

237.

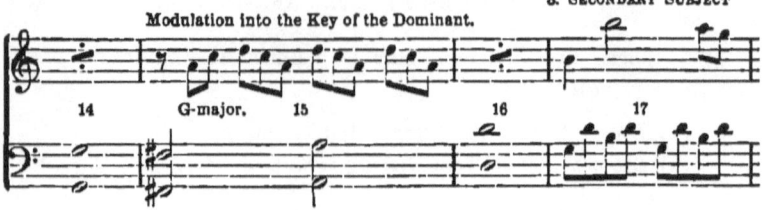

Modulation into the Key of the Dominant.

G-major.

(Song-Group).

(Perf. Cad. in G.)

4. CLOSING GROUP.

CODA.

CLOSE. Transition to the Repeat (Connecting-link).

200. The five divisions of this little model Sonatina show the following numerical proportions, which, however, are of course not given as an absolute standard:

> (1) Principal Subject....8 measures (4 + 4).
> (2) Intermediate Group..3   "   (4 × 2).
> (3) Secondary Subject...8⌣   "   (4 + 4⌣).
> (4) Closing Group.......4   "   (2 × 2).
> (5) Coda 2   "   (4 × ½).

The figures in parenthesis show that the variety of the *metrical construction* (measure-grouping) lies in the alternation of *four*-measure and of *two*-measure groups. These are the smallest groups that can be alternated.

The young composer should, in working, constantly aim at the variety resulting from such alternations.

The *rhythmical* variety lies in the use of *different kinds* of *notes* within the metrical construction; here also belongs the difference in the *points of entrance* within the measure,—for example, while the first theme enters on the first quarter-note, the second enters on the second quarter-note of the measure. This variety too is here attained with the simplest means, yet in a perfectly satisfactory manner. *The young composer should aim at this variety also, but with the same moderation and gradual progression as here,* as overloading in this respect renders a piece motley, incoherent and tedious.*

201. The structure of the foregoing model composition may be variously analyzed, from various standpoints. Thus, the piece consists,

> in *duality,* of 16 + 15 measures.
> in *triality,* of 16 + 8⌣ + 7 measures.
> in *quaternity,* of 8 + 8 + 8⌣ + 7 measures.

202. The *first theme* (principal subject) forms an *8-measure Thesis* (large phrase, see Chap. VII), to which the *intermediate group* seems at first to afford the *Antithesis;* instead of which, however, it modulates, with the first motive of the principal subject—

238.

---

* The opposite fault—rhythmical sameness—makes a piece stiff, clumsy and repulsive.

in four 2-measure sections into *G*-major by means of the Dominant-septimachord (measures 15 and 16) of that key. Herewith its *dynamic* effect is *heightened* by *forte*, its *rhythm* by the *triplet*-figure (measures 13 to 16).

203. The *second theme* (secondary subject) returns to the quieter movement in eighths and to *piano*. Its construction is that of an in-dependent tonic double-phrase (4 + 4) (Par. 40), approaching the period-form with imperfect authentic cadence in the Thesis (Par. 26).

204. The *closing group* has the form of a double-section (Par. 12), the *Coda* consists of four half-measures.

205. In the last three divisions the forms are abbreviated thus: 8, 4 and 2 measures; as also their elements: 4 measures, 2 measures, half-measures.

206. *The ruling key, from the Secondary Subject on, is the key of the DOMINANT.*

207. The *intermediate group* is developed from a motive of the first theme, here by *transposition* (measures 11, 12), *change* of *mode* (measures 13, 14), and *modulation* (15, 16). This making the most of a part of a theme is called DEVELOPMENT, or THEMATIC WORK. It will be exhaustively treated in the proper place, in its connection with the so-called DEVELOPMENT-PORTION of the *Sonata-form* (Chapters XLVIII, XLIX).

TWENTY–SECOND EXERCISE.

Compose, according to the directions above given, first parts of SONATINAS IN MAJOR.

[Take KUHLAU's Sonatina as model, though in respect to the length and construction of the separate *groups* it need not be followed absolutely. Thus, for example, the first Theme may be *tonically independent—not a Thesis*, and more frequent use may be made of *overlapping* (Chapter XIV). Former exercises may be utilized.]

CHAPTER XXXIV.

FIRST PART OF THE SONATINA IN MINOR.

208. If the Sonatina is in MINOR, the Intermediate Group modulates into the *parallel major key*, which from the second theme up to the close is the ruling key.

If, for instance, our model Sonatina (Fig. 237) were in *c*-minor, the Intermediate Group would have to lead into *E♭*-major, thus:

239.

Second Theme.

etc.

209. A very concise first part of the *minor Sonatina* is found in BEETHOVEN's *g*-minor Sonata, Op. 49, No. 1. As in KUHLAU's Sonatina, so here the principal subject forms a Thesis with Half-cadence.

240.

p

etc.
4 Measures.

I   V

The regularly beginning Antithesis is constructed as Intermediate Group, and modulates (in the manner of a half-cadence) into the Dominant of the parallel key,

241.

whereupon the second Theme (not without melodic affinity with the first) enters, is extended to over 9 measures, then repeats the last 5 measures, thus seeming disproportionately long, as against the first Theme.

242.

The closing-group also borrows its matter from the second theme:

243.

There is no *Coda*.

It may also be said, however, that *in the place of the closing*-group the last 5 measures of the second theme are repeated (especially as these form an independent phrase), and that the 5 measures above designated as closing-group may be considered as *Coda*. The scheme of the construction will then be:

> Principal Subject: 8 measures (Thesis)
> Intermediate Group: 7 measures (Antithesis).
> Secondary Subject: 9 measures.
> Closing-Group: 5 (taken from the Secondary Subject).
> Coda: ⌣5 (connecting with the Secondary Subject).

So considered, the form is better adapted as a model for the young composer.

TWENTY-THIRD EXERCISE.

Compose first parts of Sonatinas in minor.

CHAPTER XXXV.

THIRD PART OF THE SONATINA IN MAJOR.

210. The third part of the Sonatina-form differs from the first in this, that *all* the groups are in *one and the same*—the *principal—key;* otherwise, it is constructed just like the first part.

Thus, *from the second theme* on, everything is to be transposed from the Dominant to the *Tonic* (either a Fourth higher or a Fifth lower, as the esthetic effect may require).

211. The *Intermediate* group here becomes a mere *episode*, no modulation being now required. The KUHLAU Sonatina (Fig. 237) retains this episode up to the modulation note for note, and then transposes the modulatory measures 15 and 16 into the Tonic:

244.

Second Theme.

212. The *Coda* is usually, for the sake of a more decisive close, somewhat lengthened,—in the KUHLAU Sonatina by two *C*-major chords.

213. The third part is thus essentially repetition of the first, without modulation, hence it is also called REPRISE, or Repetition.

214. There would be no impropriety in beginning work on a Sonatina or Sonata with the composition of the *third* part, subsequently forming from this the first part by working over the episode between the two themes into a modulatory group.

TWENTY-FOURTH EXERCISE.

Compose the third part to the Sonatinas written for the twenty-second exercise.

215. The part which undergoes the most substantial alteration, even to the loss of an essential characteristic, is undoubtedly the *Intermediate Group*, in so far as it has in the first part the significance of *modulatory episode*, and as such appears at present superfluous. Nevertheless, it is generally retained, shorn of its modulatory character, or enriched by the interpolation of some opportune modulation, in order not to disturb the *metrical* proportion of the parts, which is on the whole more important for the form than the modulatory proportion. In the models thus far cited the Intermediate Group borrowed its matter from the principal subject, even appeared for the most part as its Antithesis. The Intermediate Group is, however, not unfrequently composed of *new* motives, especially when the principal subject is *tonically independent,* and consequently does not at once offer to the Intermediate Group a good starting-point. In this case its absence from the third part would rob the latter of an essential element of its make-up.

CHAPTER XXXVI.

THIRD PART OF THE SONATINA IN MINOR.

216. In *minor*, the third part holds strictly not only to the principal *key*, but also to the ruling *mode*. The second theme, and what follows it, undergoes therefore a much more substantial variation than in the Sonatina in *major*. For this reason the procedure mentioned in Par. 214—that of composing the third part first—would be still more advisable in the minor than in the major Sonatina.

TWENTY-FIFTH EXERCISE.

Compose third parts for the first parts of minor Sonatinas, transposing from the parallel to the tonic minor key.

217. In MOZART'S small *e*-minor Sonatina, whose principal subject, tonically independent, is given in Fig. 49 a, the course of the third part is as follows:

(This group is to be considered as perfectly independent, even though the motive with which it is entirely taken up, is drawn from the principal subject (Fig. 49 a, measures 3 and 4). Now follows in the prescribed principal key and minor mode the Secöndary Subject, in which we again only hint at the imitation in the violin).

The Closing-group is quite short;

it is followed by a *Coda* in e-minor, arpeggio, three measures.

218. In the *first part* of this Sonatina we find the Secondary Subject, Closing-group and Coda, according to rule, in the parallel key—*G*-major. *But* the Intermediate Group does not there modulate into the Dominant of *G*, but makes a half-close in e-minor, exactly as in the third part (Fig. 245).

Doubtless the composer deemed the—technically very easy—modulation not in keeping with the subject-matter, esthetically inadmissible.

He therefore interpolated in the first part between the *minor* side —Principal Subject and Intermediate Group—and the *major* side— Secondary Subject and Close—an episode of 10 measures:

Additional Intermediate Group.   Violin.

248.

etc.

which enters at once in *G*-major (the brusqueness of this modulation seemed to comport with the character of the work), and at last forming a half-cadence on the Dominant of *G*, prepares the entrance of the second theme.

But whence comes this interpolated episode? The first measure is the contrary motion of the first measure of the principal subject, the subsequent motives are taken from the sixth measure of the same.

This episode, which in the first part accomplishes what the preceding one cannot accomplish here, is wanting, accordingly, in the third part. But it is to be regarded in the first part as an anomaly, a reminiscence of the obsolete custom of once more alluding to the principal theme previously to the second theme. But perhaps Mozart had here the last part finished first in his mind.

219. It sometimes occurs, and is not considered an irregularity, that in the third part the *key* is not changed, but only the *mode*,— for example, in a piece in *g-minor*, in the third part the secondary subject, closing-group and Coda are put in *G*-major. The close, too, may likewise be made in major, or it may be led back to minor.

CHAPTER XXXVII.

OMISSION OF THE MODULATION IN THE FIRST PART.

220. In major Sonatinas the modulation into the Dominant is often replaced by a *half-cadence* on the Dominant. Thus, for instance, in the *G*-major Sonatina, Op. 49, BEETHOVEN closes in the Intermediate Group with a tolerably broad half-cadence formula, followed immediately by the Secondary Subject in the key of the Dominant:

MOZART has something similar in the *D*-major Sonatina for four hands:

221. Even in larger Sonatas, which by reason of their dimensions and subject-matter are not to be classed among Sonatinas, this easy way of introducing the new key is occasionally found. In MOZART'S *D*-major Sonata, for instance, which begins:

251.
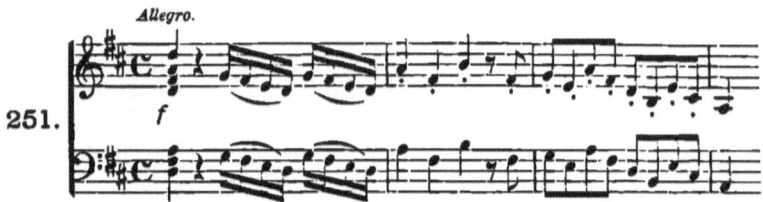

the second theme follows the Half-cadence in the same way:

252.

222. An advantage arising from this method is that in the third part of the Sonata the principal subject and intermediate group may be kept unchanged (of course not *must*).

TWENTY-SIXTH EXERCISE.

Change in this way some previous compositions.

CHAPTER XXXVIII.

SECOND PART OF THE SONATINA-FORM.

223. Between the two parts of the Sonatina which have been thus far studied enters now a *middle member*, the SECOND PART.

This second part either

(a) is concerned, as *Development-portion*, with constituent elements of the first part, thus serves for *thematic work ;* or,

(b) brings *new matter*, which, however, must not take on any complete or independent form, otherwise it would pass over to the Rondo-form ; or, finally,

(c) it brings somewhat of thematic work and somewhat of new matter.

224. The *length* of the middle-group greatly varies. In some Sonatinas it is limited to few measures, occasionally merely forming a transitional passage into the repetition ; in others again it reaches nearly the length of the first part. *As a general rule for the beginner*, the middle-group should be *shorter* than the *first part* by *about one-half, at the least*, and *about as long, at the most*.

TWENTY–SEVENTH EXERCISE.

Add, accordingly, to the Sonatinas in major and minor hitherto composed, middle-groups (Development-portions, so-called), several to each.

Combine the most successful of these exercises into complete Sonatinas.

225. The middle-group of the Sonatina forms, together with the Reprise, the *second part* of the Sonatina, which second part is in many cases repeated.

We will now study some model Sonatinas.

226. In BEETHOVEN'S *G*-major Sonatina, Op. 49, the Development-portion shows, against the 52 measures of the first part, *fourteen* measures.

The first six measures are occupied with the first theme; what
follows comprises formulas of but little moment, which serve no purpose but to lead back to the Reprise and to enhance, by their own
insignificance, the importance of the principal subject which now re-
enters.

227. In MOZART's *e*-minor Sonatina (see Fig. 245), over against the 39 measures of the first and 29 of the third part, the second part shows 15 measures. The beginning finds its *starting-point* in the principal theme, the rest is free, likewise of formular character, but of greater significance.

228. Both Sonatinas therefore show, in the middle-group, at least *thematic reminiscence*, though independent construction predominates.

229. In the Development-portion of BEETHOVEN'S *g*-minor Sonatina, on the contrary, thematic treatment predominates. The very introduction, a modulation into *E♭*-major, starts out from the second theme (see Fig. 242):

255.

Hereupon follows an entirely new episode of a 2 × 4-measure phrase, tonically rounded off in *E♭*-major.

256.

The next eighteen measures, however, belong thematically to the second theme, which, *itself*, as we have seen (Par. 209), is in this composition thematically akin to the first theme.

230. In our little *model Sonatina by* KUHLAU, on the contrary, the construction is *perfectly free*. Here the second part begins with the development of the new rhythmic motive—

borrowing from the opening only the unimportant accompaniment-figure in the left hand—into a four-measure phrase; then in rhythmic variation—

after four more measures a so-called *deceptive cadence* * in *A♭*-major, which leads to a half-cadence on the dominant (major) of *c*-minor, thence in commonplace scale-passages, etc., to the Reprise. These passages may, of course, be regarded as thematically akin to the closing-group and Coda of the first part, if indeed anything so commonplace and insignificant can lay claim to thematic character. This insignificance, commonplaceness and formularity of the elaborations, far from being a reproach to the compositions here cited, which are all *perfect models of their kind*, are essential characteristics of the Sonatina, in which the development-portion should not have a detrimental effect upon the repetition of the themes in the Reprise. The whole development is here *in a certain sense* a Cadenza on the septimachord leading from the dominant to the tonic, and thus the dominant harmony counterpoises the entirely tonic character of the Reprise.

---

* This term for a progression of the Dominant Triad or Septimachord to another chord than the expected *Tonic* harmony, is, as LOBE justly observes, inappropriate, seeing that the unexpected chord may be a *dissonance*, in which case there is, of course, no *Cadence* in the proper sense, nor even a *resolution* of the Dominant harmony. In the interests of a more exact musical terminology I venture to make this proposition: Let the progression of the Dominant harmony (a) to that of the *Tonic* be called its *principal resolution;* (b) to *any other major* or *minor Triad*, a *secondary resolution;* and (c) to any *dissonance*, an *unexpected progression*, or something similar, the important word being "progression," as distinguished from "resolution."

B. THE SONATA.

231. By *enlargement* of the parts, and consequently of the whole, from the Sonatina arises the SONATA. The *proportion* between the parts remains the same, in respect as well of modulation as of dimensions and metrical structure in general. The GRAND SONATA, too, is nothing more than a Sonata, of unusually great dimensions.

CHAPTER XXXIX.

ENLARGEMENT OF THE PRINCIPAL SUBJECT.

(a) BY REPETITION.

232. If the *principal subject* is of considerable significance, especially of energetic rhythmical construction, it may be *repeated*, the close of the repetition forming at the same time the starting-point for what follows. For example:

This noted theme from BEETHOVEN's Sonata (pathétique) Op. 13, is adapted for a repetition, on account of the forcible *contrast* between its two parts, and it requires this repetition because, in the quick *tempo* prescribed, *once* is not enough to make the proper impression. But in repeating it makes a half-cadence, and this is the starting-point for the intermediate group or link-episode.

258.

In the $E\flat$-major Sonata, Op. 31, the principal subject is repeated an Octave higher, each time with a complete close in the *tonic*.

(b) By Addition.

233. The principal subject may be enlarged also by the *addition* of another group, forming, so to speak, an afterlude, coda or refrain to the first,—a favorite form with Mozart.

In the $E\flat$-major Symphony of this master the principal subject forms the following 14 + 14⌣ measure period, here given, for saving room, in the most meagre melodic abridgment:

259.

On the final measure (lacking here) of this tender subject **now** enters a fiery *forte*, after the manner of "Tutti," of 18 measures,

and on the last chord of which the intermediate group (m
episode) begins.

The 8 measures, too, which in the Pathetic Sonata follow
tition of the principal subject, may be considered as adde
latter as a kind of cadence-formula (organ-point ending wit
cadence), so that in this case we have both repetition *and* ad

It is certain that in the c♯-minor Sonata (Op. 27), in th
the organ-point on the Dominant—

which also is substantially a lengthened half-cadence, is to be regarded as an addition to the principal subject.*

234. The above example from MOZART is, esthetically, essentially distinguished from the examples first cited by the circumstance that the second theme is followed by a more delicate echo, which seems to die away entirely in the Coda. The smaller form of the parts implies the proportionate shortness of the whole.

By a kind of *Prelude*, BEETHOVEN enlarges the theme of the great B♭-major Sonata, Op. 106 (which see).

(c) BY PERIOD-FORMATION.

235. The Period, being a complete musical thought, is for this reason not so well adapted to be a member of a group forming a Sonata. For the most part the principal subject constitutes only the *Thesis* of a period, to which is joined—*instead* of the Antithesis and with its motives—the intermediate group; thus the latter, instead of closing periodically with the Thesis, reaches over into the sphere of another key.

---

* We have here an example of those original and energetic cadence-formulas which BEETHOVEN substituted for the trivial, common-property cadences in use before his time.

236. Nevertheless we have above already had an example from MOZART, in which a long period united with another thought to form a principal subject. There are also extended periods which alone occupy the entire space of the principal subject.

We give here two examples, one from BEETHOVEN with considerably *shortened,* one from MOZART with considerably *lengthened* Antithesis, both in the most meagre melodic abridgment only, leaving the filling up to the student's memory.

263.

The thought closing in the 8th measure, and consisting of four dimeters (forming a *quadruple section,* see Par. 13), is here followed by a second thought, without any thematic relationship to the first, but forming esthetically a most decided contrast to it, and ending with a half-cadence; thus we have a 16-measure Thesis. The Antithesis, which at least suggests the motive of the first Thesis, consists of only 2 × 4 measures (double phrase), but is extended by a small Coda to 12 measures. This Coda is immediately followed by the intermediate group.

237. We have here, moreover, an excellent example of the *large three-part period* (Chapter VIII), which, like the example from MOZART (Fig. 57), has two Theses.

Here we see the very first four measures ending with a half-cadence, which seems to characterize them as Thesis of a period. The continuation, however, does not take period-shape, but again makes a half-cadence (by means of the augmented Sextachord). Esthetically, too, the character of Antithesis is wanting, on account of the rhythm pressing forward as it does, although the motives thus rhythmically enlivened are those of the first Thesis. It is now that the Antithesis proper begins, which embraces sixteen measures as against eight of the Thesis. The enlargement is effected through the agency of the motive ⌐a⌐, which is four times repeated and leads to a thematically free close.

238. By means of the shortening and lengthening of the Anti-thesis, as illustrated in the foregoing examples, the period loses that independent, complete-in-itself character which is repugnant to the Sonata-form.

239. In the *c*-minor Symphony BEETHOVEN constructs, after a 5-measure Introduction, an extended Thesis of 16 measures. To this corresponds—after 3 measures of introduction—an Antithesis of 20 measures. The enlargement by 4 measures is made out of the motive of the Thesis:

265.

which in the Antithesis is transformed and developed in the following manner:

266.

Beginning of the Intermediate Group.

This principal subject thus exhibits a large period, embracing—not counting the 8 measures of introduction—36 measures. The close of this period is, however, by means of the division and the impetuous forward movement of the motives, rhythmically so constructed that the period does not seem to end, but to incessantly press onward. The *great art* in the Sonata-form is, in fact, *to avoid* CADENCES *by means of the rhythmical construction.*

240. There are, of course, *other ways* of extending the principal subject. To find these in the works of the masters, and to imitate them, will be easy to the young composer who has carefully attended to the foregoing explanations.

TWENTY-EIGHTH EXERCISE.

Compose, according to the methods here explained, enlarged principal subjects of the Sonata-form up to the entrance of the Intermediate Group. For this purpose utilize, as far as possible, material already on hand.

The student is *especially cautioned* not to compose these exercises in the form of meagre *melodic abridgment* (as in many of our illustrations), afterwards adding the *harmonization,*—but, like a true artist, to have constantly in his mind at the same time *melody and harmony as forming a whole,* as also the presentation of his ideas by means of the *particular instrument* (or instruments) which he chooses for the purpose.

Here follow some examples from BEETHOVEN, given in their entirety, in order to stimulate the student's imagination.

MODELS.

PRINCIPAL SUBJECT, *F*-MAJOR QUARTET, OP. 18.

Coda to Antithesis, quasi 2d Antithesis.

PRINCIPAL SUBJECT, *C*-MAJOR QUARTET, OP. 59.

PRINCIPAL SUBJECT, *a*-MINOR (KREUTZER) SONATA.

269.

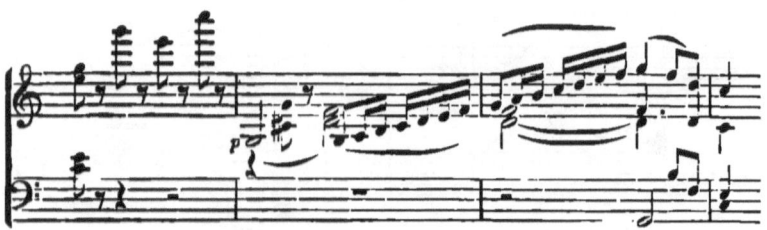

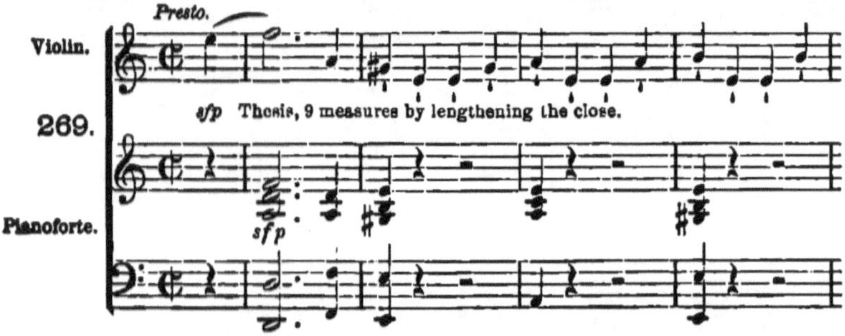

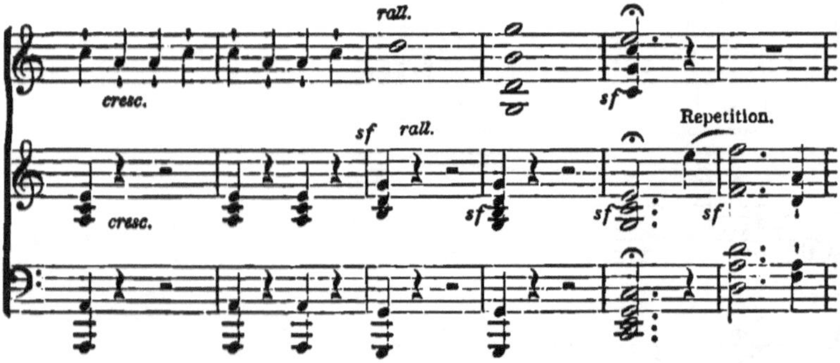

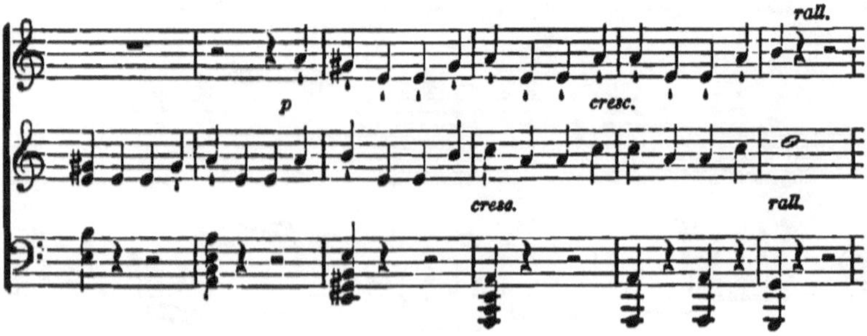

Beginning of the Intermediate Group.

CHAPTER XL.

THE INTERMEDIATE GROUP.

241. The Intermediate Group is, as we have seen, in the first part of the Sonatina-form of a *modulatory* character, as bringing in the new key (that of the secondary subject). The modulation is in this case of a *more or less* radical character.

(a) In the case of the *Sonatina* we saw (Chapter XXXVII) that the secondary subject may enter in its new key (that of the Dominant), without previous *modulation* into that key, *i. e.*, after a *half-cadence* on the Dominant. This seldom occurs in the larger *Sonata*, yet it is sometimes ·found, especially in MOZART. In this case, then, the easy task of the intermediate group is to end with a half-cadence.

(b) The modulation is more *decisive* when the new key is introduced by means of its *dominant-septimachord* (as in KUHLAU'S model Sonatina).

(c) But the most decisive and most usual way, in large Sonatas, of introducing the new key (Dominant) for the second theme, is by means of the *dominant of the dominant*, which, for want of a better name and in imitation of the German designation (Wechseldominant) we will call RECIPROCAL DOMINANT. To change, for instance, from *C*-major to *G*-major, first modulate to *D*-major, then back, as it were, to *G*-major. Or, to go from *a*-minor to *e*-minor, modulate first to *B*-major (dominant of *e*-minor). To go from *c*-minor to *E♭*-major, modulate first to *B♭*-major, dominant of the parallel key.

Thus MOZART, for instance, in the *g*-minor Symphony, though he has already reached the parallel key, yet modulates into its dominant before bringing in the secondary subject in *B♭*·major.

270.

etc.

242. A method occupying middle ground between the last two methods (**b** and **c**), is that of making a *perfect cadence in the new key,* as in BEETHOVEN'S *D*-major Sonata, Op. 10.

271.

243. The *Intermediate Group itself,* in its enlarged form in the Sonata is, as to its construction, either (**A**) *thematically borrowed from the principal subject ;* or (**B**) *independent ;* or (**C**) *partly borrowed, partly independent.*

A.

244. The intermediate group follows the principal subject as *Antithesis* or *Repetition,* and leads its motives into the new key.

So BEETHOVEN in the Finale of the *c♯*-minor Sonata, where the principal subject, as Thesis, closes with the Coda given in Fig. 261. The *Antithesis* now seems to enter, at least the beginning at once re-appears :

But, instead of returning to the principal key, a modulation is made with the chief motive, which finally puts on a more tender form, to the key of the dominant—*g♯*-minor, in which the second theme at once enters.

245. If the principal subject makes a *tonic close*, the place of the *Antithesis* is taken by the *Repetition*, as in MOZART'S *a*-minor Sonata. The principal subject is an 8-measure phrase, on the last measure of which the repetition, and with it the intermediate group enters.

Repetition and Intermediate Group.

Just as, in the example from BEETHOVEN, the modulatory Anti thesis was *preceded* by a cadence-formula on the dominant (Fig. 261) so in this example from MOZART the *repetition* is *followed* by a simila formula on the dominant of the new key just reached.

In the E♭-major Sonata, Op. 31, the intermediate group, afte the repetition of the principal subject (Par. 232), sets out with th chief motive of the latter, finally making with the second motive th prescribed modulation.

B.

246. The intermediate group is constructed from *independen motives*. It is thus, for instance, in MOZART'S E♭-major Symphony The principal subject of the first *Allegro* (Figs. 259, 260) is imme diately followed by the intermediate group with the motive—

This same section is repeated five times, modulating:

establishes itself in F-major on an organ-point,

and then, with an entirely new motive,

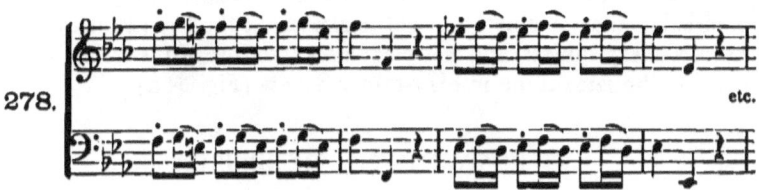

278.

etc.

passes into *Bb*-major, to lead into the secondary subject.

In the *Don Giovanni* overture the episode between the principal and the secondary subject is *quite independent.*

C.

247. The intermediate group makes the principal subject its *starting-point,* but passes on to *independent* construction.

In MOZART'S *g*-minor Symphony the chief subject takes the form of an enlarged Thesis of 16 measures. This is followed by the Antithesis:

279.

New Thought in the Episode.

Modulation to *Bb*-major.

Modulation to the Dominant of the parallel.

(Secondary Subject.)

Here we see the episode begin as Antithesis and pass on to independent construction before leading into the secondary subject. It is remarkable that this new thought is already in the key (*Bb*-major) of the secondary subject and yet *modulates* into it. MOZART has done precisely the same thing in his *c*-minor Sonata (Fig. 54 a).

TWENTY-NINTH EXERCISE.

Add to the principal subjects of the preceding exercise, according to the methods here laid down, episodes leading, in either one of the ways mentioned under (B) and (C), pp. 194, 195, into the key of the second theme.

CHAPTER XLI.

THE SECONDARY SUBJECT (SONG-GROUP).

248. The second theme generally forms the strongest contrast to the first which is found in the whole movement, in particular it takes on a more *songful* character when the first theme was very profuse in *figuration*. In other respects its construction shows quite as much variety as that of the first theme, or even more may be allowed, under the stimulating influence of the preceding development.

249. The *extent* of the secondary subject is, as a rule, somewhat greater than that of the principal subject *without* episode, but considerably less than that of the principal subject *with* episode. We give below two "Secondary Subjects" as specimens of construction.

250. The secondary subject must always form a perfect cadence in its principal key, which is, as we have seen, in *major*, that of the *Dominant;* in *minor*, the *parallel* (major), or the *minor* key of the *Dominant*.

[The student should analyze the first movements of the best-known Symphonies, Sonatas, and Quartets of BEETHOVEN, of the last three Symphonies of MOZART (*g*-minor, *E*b-major, *C*-major), and of the other sonata-form compositions of these masters, and of HAYDN, with a view to studying the construction of the secondary themes and their relation to the principal themes.]

BEETHOVEN. FINALE OF THE c♯-MINOR SONATA.

Second Theme. g♯-minor.

280.

MOZART. FIRST MOVEMENT OF THE c-MINOR SONATA.

Second Theme. E♭-major.

BEETHOVEN.

MOZART.

BEETHOVEN.

MOZART.

BEETHOVEN.

MOZART.

We see that here also, and even more decidedly than in the princi-pal subject, both great masters do *not* hold fast to the motives of the first measures, but drop them after one repetition and pass on to new motives.   But the theme itself makes a perfect close.

THIRTIETH EXERCISE.

Compose the Secondary Subjects to the previous exercises. Utilize, as much as possible, such material already on hand as is suitable—not in order to spare the exercise of the imagination, but because we are concerned here with formal construction, not with invention, and taste, not genius, is being cultivated.

251. An example, in which an episode (with new motives) is interpolated between the secondary subject (16-measure period) and the subsequent closing-group, is found in the *F*-major Sonata by MOZART, the principal subject of which is given in Fig. 262.

281.

etc. up to

etc.

252. Still more notable is the episode interpolated, in the KREUTZER Sonata, between the second theme and the closing-group, which once more goes through the whole modulation. In the former case it is admissible to regard the new episode as a quite *special kind* of Thesis of the closing-group; in the latter case the assumption of a special kind of Antithesis to the second theme, instead of a second episode, is conceivable.

CHAPTER XLII.

THE CLOSING-GROUP.

253. Esthetically, the closing-group has, as a rule, somewhat of the character of the principal subject, especially when the latter was of a rather lively figuration. Its dimensions are such as to pretty nearly sustain the equilibrium in the *duality* (Par. 195) of the first part of the Sonata-form.

254. Technically, the character of the closing-group is on the whole that of a prolonged cadence-formula on a melodic motive. The closing-group is sometimes repeated, sometimes composed of several different motives.

The model for this part of the Sonata-form is the closing-group of BEETHOVEN'S c#-minor Sonata. It follows immediately after the second theme and is climacterically *repeated*.

The closing-group in MOZART'S *g*-minor Symphony is *composite*, and shows three divisions:

255. Sometimes the closing-group seems to be only a Coda to the secondary subject, as in BEETHOVEN's *e*-minor Sonata.

CHAPTER XLIII.

THE CODA.

256. The Coda, already known to us as fifth part of the Sonatina-form, is sometimes limited in the *Sonata-form also* to a few chords, yet it occasionally has also larger dimensions, and even is composite. A model, for clear separation of the parts and normal structure of them, is here again the c♯-minor Sonata, in which the closing-group given in Fig. 282 is followed by this thought as Coda (Construction: 2 × 2 + 2 × 1):

285.

An example of a Coda consisting of two different parts is found in MOZART's *F*-major Sonata (Fig. 262):

286.

Here are some examples of usual construction:

BEETHOVEN. *c-minor Symphony.*

287.

MOZART. *g-minor Symphony.*

288.

BEETHOVEN's *e*-minor Sonata, Op. 90, has only two chords as Coda,—they follow what is given in Fig. 284. Exceptionally (very rarely) the Coda is altogether wanting.

CHAPTER XLIV.

THE CONNECTING LINK.

257. In the *Sonatina* we have seen, that for leading into the repetition or continuation a *connecting link* follows mediately or immediately the close of the first part (see Fig. 237). The necessity for such a link arises from the relation of the close to the repetition (or, as the case may be, to the continuation into the second part).

Thus MOZART in the *c*-minor Sonata (Fig. 54) utilizes for both purposes the figure borrowed from the principal subject:

289.

[The first time repetition follows, the 2d time development.]

To the Coda in the Finale of the *c♯*-minor Sonata (Fig. 285) BEETHOVEN appends the following link:

290.

The Repetition here begins.

This way of constructing the connecting link, viz: out of motives of the principal subject, is, especially with BEETHOVEN and his successors, very frequent, almost the usual practice.

In the *e*-minor Sonata for piano and violin MOZART uses as connecting-link even a *Canon* formed from the principal theme:

which, in the third part, is thus repeated in the principal key:

THIRTY–FIRST EXERCISE.

Complete the Sonata movements already begun by adding closing-group and Coda; also, as may be required, connecting-link for the repetition.

[By means of the exercises of this Part the student must have composed many first part of the Sonata-form. We now proceed to the easy work of constructing the third part (Reprise).]

CHAPTER XLV.

THIRD PART OF THE SONATA-FORM.

258. The third part is formed from the first by avoiding the change of key. The process of construction is just as in the case of the Sonatina. The groups maintain on the whole the same dimensions, though abbreviations and extensions in particular cases are, of course, not excluded.

259. On account of the omission of the modulation the intermediate group between the first and the second theme may, strictly speaking, be dispensed with, as indeed is sometimes done in the Reprise. Thus, for instance, the c♯-minor Sonata in the third part closes the principal subject exactly as in the first, viz: on a half-cadence with organ-point and pause ; but then—skipping the intermediate group—at once enters upon the secondary subject,—

293.

after which everything follows the regular course.

In the *d*-minor Sonata, Op. 31, also, in the third part, the intermediate group of the first part is altogether wanting; it had, however, in the development-portion (second part), or rather *as* development, already been repeated entire.

260. As a rule, on the other hand, the intermediate group is retained by the great masters of the Sonata-form, and often exploited for thematic work, and then sometimes even enlarged.

MOZART, in his later works, is fond of treatment of this kind, as, for instance, in the *g*-minor Symphony, where the characteristic motive of the intermediate group ⌐a⌐ —

294.

(See Fig. 279.)

is in an interesting manner harmonically and contrapuntally developed, and, as against the first part, lengthened by 21 measures. In the celebrated *Finale*, fugued in quadruple counterpoint, of the great *C*-major Symphony, he uses this place for an equally interesting *Stretto* through the circle of Fourths.

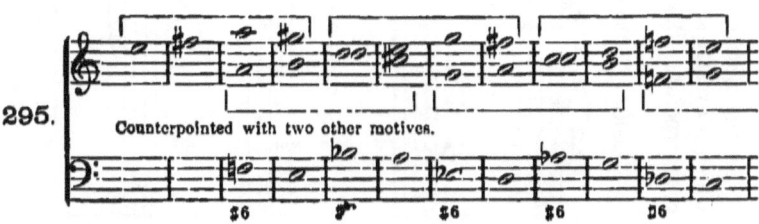

295.

Counterpointed with two other motives.

In the first movement of the same *C*-major Symphony Mozart likewise introduces at this place a thought which is exactly as long as the corresponding one in the first part, but intensified by means of modulation and counterpoint. Both these thoughts are here placed in juxtaposition for the sake of comparison.

296.   In the First Part.

in the Third Part.

This procedure is recommended to the young composer also. He should retain the intermediate group, judiciously enlarging and enriching it.

THIRTY–SECOND EXERCISE.

Compose, accordingly, the third part of Sonatas already written.

CHAPTER XLVI.

MODULATORY LICENSE.

261. In Sonatas in *minor* whose *second* theme, with the subsequent closing-group and Coda, will not bear transposition into the *minor* mode, the *major mode of the principal key* is substituted. This modulatory license is found in many compositions by HAYDN, but a striking example of it is seen in BEETHOVEN's *c*-minor Symphony. Here the second theme—

297.

would not allow transposition into minor, as it would thereby entirely lose its character; it therefore now appears in the major mode of the principal key—*C:*

298.

in which the closing-group also then follows, whose triumphant fi
character is likewise repugnant to the minor mode:

299.

That the movement, notwithstanding, closes in *minor,* will
accounted for farther on (see Par, 283).

CHAPTER XLVII.

MODIFICATIONS OF PARTICULAR GROUPS IN THE THIRD PART.

A. Modifications of the Principal Theme.

262. In the *d*-minor Sonata BEETHOVEN shortens the *first the*
by the greater part of its figurate matter, while he lengthens it by 1
Largo-recitatives:

300.

He then, with a few measures of modulation,

301.

passes on, omitting the intermediate group, to the second theme, which now appears in *d*-minor.

302.

In the Pathetic Sonata he forms from the second part of the first theme a modulatory group,

303.

which here takes the place of the intermediate group of the first part.

B. MODIFICATIONS OF THE INTERMEDIATE GROUP.

263. The *Intermediate Group* is sometimes *itself transposed*, in order to remain *unaltered*. Thus, for instance, in the first movement of MOZART's *Eb*-major Symphony, the first theme is led in the third part to a close in the *Subdominant*, in order that the unaltered intermediate group may close in the Tonic. (Tonic to Subdominant, equivalent to Dominant to Tonic).

C. MODIFICATIONS OF THE SECONDARY SUBJECT.

264. The *Secondary Subject* appears, in the Pathetic Sonata, at first in the key of the *Subdominant*, and not till thirteen measures later in that of the *Tonic*.

304.

We observe, in passing, that this theme in the *first* part does not enter in the (regular) *major* key—*E♭*, but in the *homonymic minor key—e♭*, and makes only its *close* in major.

D. MODIFICATIONS OF CLOSING-GROUP AND CODA.

265. The *Closing-group* and *Coda* are, for the sake of a more decided close, often modified by an *extension,* which is sometimes shorter, sometimes longer, and exceptionally attains the proportions of a quite new and comprehensive part of the close. Illustrations of this are found in BEETHOVEN's "Eroica" and Ninth Symphonies.

CHAPTER XLVIII.

THE DEVELOPMENT-PORTION.

266. The development-portion of the large Sonata should occupy itself exclusively, or almost exclusively, with the themes and motives of the first part; where it does not, its contents are not up to the requirements of the large Sonata-form, and this form loses somewhat of its importance.

267. In the master-pieces of MOZART and HAYDN the development is for the most part considerably shorter than the two other parts, say about half as long, while in BEETHOVEN'S works it attains to the dimensions of the other parts, sometimes even is longer. This is explained by the fact that BEETHOVEN'S genius found its greatest resource in THEMATIC WORK, whilst the two masters first named occupied themselves more with the technical construction of the whole.

THEMATIC WORK.

268. The expression "thematic work" embraces everything that can possibly be made out of a theme, by harmonization, figuration, variation, counterpoint, instrumentation, in the broadest sense of each of these terms.

269. In the works of the *classical* masters of our instrumental music the employment of *counterpoint* * is limited, as a rule, to *imitation*, the *fugue* and the *canon* being only *exceptionally* introduced.† Thus MOZART, in the "Magic Flute" overture, and BEETHOVEN, in the overture "The Consecration of the House," touch upon the fugue-form; the latter composer, in the *c*-minor Sonata for violin and piano, upon the canon. The finale of MOZART'S great *C*-major Symphony is based even on a quadruple counterpoint, and BEETHOVEN'S Symphonies and other instrumental works exhibit small canons. Yet these are, in proportion to the majority of the works, only *exceptions*; exceptions which show how far thematic work *can* go in this direction when it is requisite, and how completely the composer should be equipped for every emergency.

CHAPTER XLIX.

THEMATIC WORK IN THE DEVELOPMENT-PORTION.

270. In the development-portion the thematic work must be done according to *system*, not capriciously springing from one thought to another without any method.

---

* Excepting, of course, in those works which are professedly written in contrapuntal style throughout, such as independent fugues, canons, etc., with which we are here not directly concerned.

† In BEETHOVEN'S *A*-major Sonata the whole development-portion takes the form of a *fugue*, whose subject is drawn from the first theme.

271. The special difficulty of the development is that it begins modulating in the key in which it has to end, viz.: that of the Dominant. To obviate this difficulty and gain room for the modulation, the masters occasionally open the development-portion with a modulation into a remote key. MOZART, in the first movement of the *C*-major Symphony, modulates directly into *E♭*-major, and that in *unisono:*

and, in the *g*-minor Symphony, with a few chords from *B♭*-major (parallel key) into *f♯*-minor:

BEETHOVEN, in the *D*-major Sonata, Op. 10, begins the development in *B♭*-major:

MENDELSSOHN, in the *a*-minor Symphony, introduces the second part (development) in a manner as original as it is charming, by letting the tonic of *e*-minor, with which the first part ends, remain, and the horns sound against it the *major Fifth c♯—g♯*, with doubling in the Octave.

If this *e* were tonic of *E-major*, the entrance of the *c♯*-minor Tri
would be quite commonplace and without effect.

272. The *principal rules* for the development are these: O
should not take up a motive, not knowing what to do with it; n
should a motive be given up till it has been thoroughly exploited.
motive, once abandoned, should not be resumed, unless, by means
contrast or climax, with greatly *heightened effect*.

273. In the *modulation* there should be *order*, not purposele
wandering from one key to another; especially, pains should be take
to avoid the key of the *Dominant* (of the principal key) before th
end of the development. The close of the development is preem
nently suitable for an *organ-point on the Dominant*.

274. The syntax (so to speak) of the development-portion shou
be according to strict form, as in the other parts; here, however, th
smaller forms predominate, and their construction is quite independe
of any tonic, this being the place for *free modulation*.

275. A sequence-like repetition of smaller groups may easi
appear trifling or pedantic (of course, however, much depends on th
kind of sequence *).

276. On the other hand, the repetition of large and very artisti
ally elaborated groups, in another key, perhaps also with sligh
variations, is of decided advantage to the development-portion,
promoting the greater clearness of its form. Examples are found
BEETHOVEN's great Symphonies, especially in the first movement
the Ninth.

277. There is no symphonic movement which illustrates th
exploitation of the elements of the Sonata-form in a more succin
and striking manner than does the first movement of the *c*-min
Symphony. Of the motives of the first part the following are em
ployed in it for development: the *chief motive:*

309.

the thematically allied motive:

---

* In WAGNER's works are harmonic sequences which are surely anything b
dry and pedantic.

the first half of the same:

the enlargement of the chief motive:

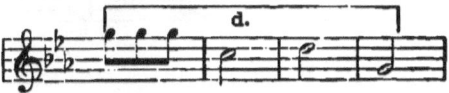

the 2d and 3d measures of the same:

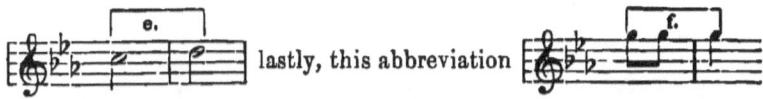

lastly, this abbreviation

of the chief motive.   The following is the scheme of the development:
motive **a** forms the introduction (measures 1—4) and double-phrase
in *f*-minor (5—13); motive **b** appears twice (13—18); motive **c**
modulates (18—21) from *f*-minor into the (major) dominant of
c-minor, with the counterpoint—

here a half-cadence formula (22—25), then to the dominant of *g*-minor
(25—29); half-cadence formula (30—33); then, in direct and contrary
motion

(34—44) to the diminished septimachord on $\mathrm{\not{V}II}°$ of *g*-minor.   Here,
chief motive **a** enlarged:

twice (44—51); the same motive in its original rhythm, once (51—
52); ditto, abbreviated (motive **f**), twice (53—55); motive **d** alternating with **f** (55—68); motive **f** (68—71); motive **e** (72—85); ditto,
with modification of pitch (86—103); motive **d** (104—108); motive
e, as merely alternation of two half-notes (109—116); motive **a**,
partly entire, partly shortened (116—124), leads into the introduction
(124—128); at measure 129 the Reprise begins.

278. Mozart, in the *C*-major Symphony, No. 1, introduces the development with the *unisono* change to *Eb*-major given in Fig. 305, and repeats the closing-group in this key. To the last motive of the closing-group,

310.

he appends a modulation, transferring the motive from the flute and bassoon to the violins; then, alternating between first and second violins and basses together with viola, leads, with the contrasting rhythms

into *g*-minor. Here he constructs a two-voiced free canon between violins and basses upon the first half of the motive, with temporary modification of it:

again closes in *g*-minor, and in the last measure brings in the lengthened closing-motive, as it appeared at first:

this is followed by an *imitation* of the last measure, forming a half-cadence on the major Dominant of *a*-minor. This dominant is changed, by the progression of the lower voices, into the dominant of *F*-major :

Thus far, therefore, the development is occupied exclusively with the closing-group of the first part, principally with its last motive. The first theme now enters in *F*-major, and modulates, with the counterpoint which it already had in the first part, into *a*-minor, and forms here with its first motive a group—strongly syncopated by the full orchestra against the first and second violins—

of 10 measures, which closes in *G*-major. Hereupon repetition of the close in *piano* with the motive of the closing-group:

Then 6 measures of organ-point on *g*, as dominant of the principal key, with the same motive of the closing-group and with a little canon :

leading into the Reprise. In this development, therefore, the one motive of the closing-group predominates throughout, it forms the first modulatory group and the close, and in doing this it twice involves th measure which originally preceded it. Between these two formation lies the elaboration of the first theme, especially of its first motive The modulation leads on the one side to $E\flat$-major, f-minor, on th other to a-minor, E-major, thus moves in seven or eight places of th circle of Fifths (Quint-circle).

THIRTY-THIRD EXERCISE.

Compose developments for former exercises, first after the two model given, then after a well-considered plan of your own.

CHAPTER L.

THE SONATA-FORM AS A WHOLE.

279. The *main purpose* of this work having been accomplished i the production of complete Sonata-movements, it seems to be time t call attention to the *licenses* which the masters have taken in usin this *chief form of all instrumental music*, without abrogating any c its essential conditions. We shall moreover notice those modification of the form which arise from connection with other movements, an finally consider the influence of thematic work on formal structure.

A. LICENSE OF MODULATION.

280. The *regular* change of key in the first part is, as we hav seen, in *major*, into the key of the *Dominant ;* in *minor*, into th *parallel* (major), or the (minor) key of the *Dominant.* As a triflin exception we have seen in the *Pathetic Sonata* the entrance of th secondary subject in the *minor* mode of the *parallel* (but with clos in major).* More important exceptions to the rule of modulatio are found in the later works of BEETHOVEN and his successors.

---

* In the *Sonata appassionata*, Op. 57, the second theme is constructed, accord ing to the rule, in *major* (Par. 208), but the closing-group and coda in *minor*, s that the first part ends in ab-minor. Thus the second theme seems to shine wit a mild radiance though the gloom of the whole movement.

In the Grand Sonata in *C*-major,

311.

the secondary subject—

312.

and the closing-group—

313.

are in *E*-major, whilst the Coda modulates from *a*-minor ʋ
e-minor :

314.

In the Grand Sonata in $B\flat$ (Fig. 104), O
$B\flat$, Op. 97 (Fig. 8), the modulation is into G
in the first part from the second theme on.
Op. 111, $A\flat$-major, parallel of the Subdomir
$E\flat$-major, the parallel; so, too, in the Nint
takes the place of F-major. The eight ot
master are regular as regards modulation.

Of BEETHOVEN's earlier works the C-majc
shows the modulation to A-major with close i
Sonata, Op. 31, the modulation to B-major, b

In the $E\flat$-major quartet, Op. 127, the m
It is left to the student's examination of ϵ
other examples.

281. It sometimes occurs that the secon
in a more remote key, but directly discovers t
on its own appointed key, and in this key pur
course; as, for instance, in BEETHOVEN's $B\flat$-1
violin, and piano-forte, also in the F-major S

282. On the other hand, a case may be c
theme enters in the *principal key* (thus wi
only later, after the manner of antithesis, lea
(in this case the parallel). This instance, wh
probably unique, is found in the first movemc
quintet; the large period given in Fig. 264, 1
theme, is followed by a group of six measure

but a cadence-formula (in the Tonic). The second theme now enters in *g*-minor, above an extremely simple accompaniment-figure,

315.

and forms a half-cadence looking towards *B♮*-major, which, after touching the major chord of *C* (reciprocal dominant of *B♭*), leads into the tonic Triad of *B♭*, in which the antithesis now enters.

316.

The course of this technically important secondary subject in the Reprise confirms the explanation given ; it is here represented in melodic abridgment, for the sake of comparison :

317.

The Closing-group, also considerably extended, here follows.

REMARK.—Here the second theme has *in a certain sense attracted to itself* the intermediate group (which otherwise belongs to the first theme), and made it its *Thesis* (just as the intermediate group generally enters as Antithesis of the first theme). The *dimensions* also correspond to this view of the case, as the division of the first part by two (duality, see Par. 195), falls upon the half-cadence which brings in the new key.

283. We have seen (Par. 261) that *minor* Sonatas often have, in the third part, the second theme and what belongs to it in the *major mode* of the principal key. If, however, the character of the first theme (in minor) strongly predominates, it must be restored, together with the original minor mode, by means of a Coda, so that the close of the movement may be in unity with the rest. Such a Coda is, in view of its purpose, of course too important to be despatched in a few notes; rather, it takes the form of a new part. It is thus—to take a

striking example—in BEETHOVEN's c-minor Symphony (1st movement), in which, after a perfect close in C-major a modulation is made
into c-minor, and a close is formed whose dimensions are equal to those
of any other part of the movement.

B.   CHANGE OF PLACE OF THE GROUPS.

284. *Occasionally* the principal subject appears once more at the
end of the whole movement, that is, when it seems to have a very
special interest.   But it *frequently* exchanges its appointed place at
the *beginning* of the Reprise for a place at the *close* of the latter; as,
for instance, in MOZART's *D*-major Sonata ·

318.

in which the lively figuration of the development would act injuriously
on the principal subject if following too closely, since the latter also
is of a lively figurated character.

285. In BEETHOVEN's *d*-minor Sonata the *intermediate group* of
the first part is taken up into the *development*, of which it constitutes
the essential elements.   Hence this intermediate group is *altogether
lacking* in the *Reprise.*

C.   INTRODUCTION AND FINAL CODA.

286. Not unfrequently the *Allegro* of the Sonata is preceded by
a slow *Introduction*, an *Adagio*, a *Largo, Lento*, etc., as, for example,
MOZART's *E♭*-major Symphony, BEETHOVEN's Pathetic Sonata, and
many other works.   This introduction sometimes influences the
Sonata, which borrows motives from it.   In MOZART's *E♭*-major
Symphony the figure (in sixteenths) of the intermediate group

319.

is borrowed from the introductory *Adagio ;* in the Pathetic Sonata
the *Allegro* is repeatedly interrupted by the *Grave* of the introduction, and this place in the development—

320

can be traced back to the motive (in the introduction),

which motive, again, is formed from the first measure of the introduction :

321.

287. That the *Coda,* at the *repetition,* is often somewhat lengthened, we already know (Par. 212). This lengthening, however, sometimes reaches the dimensions of a large thematically elaborated closing-
group, especially in BEETHOVEN's compositions.

288. A moderately lengthened Coda is found in MOZART's *g*-
minor Symphony. In BEETHOVEN's *c♯*-minor Sonata, on the other
hand, the Coda has almost the dimensions of the Reprise itself, draw-
ing its material from the first and second themes and the coda-group,
and working it up with great power and brilliancy. In the *c*-minor
Symphony we have already seen (Par. 261) the second theme in the
repetition closing in the major mode of the principal key, and followed
by an extended thematic Coda in *c*-minor, which ends the movement
in this key. Nearly all of BEETHOVEN's Symphonies, also many of

his Sonatas, quartets and other compositions, show this extension of the Coda, proving how rich this master was in resources of thematic development and climax.

REMARK.—The occurrence of *different Tempi* within the Sonata-form is illustrated in BEETHOVEN's *d*-minor Sonata, whose principal theme has two *tempi*. In a Duo-sonata in *C*-major by MOZART the principal theme is in Adagio,

the secondary theme in Allegro,

289.   **D.** THE THEMATIC WORK

is extended also to *other parts* of the Sonata-form than the intermediate group, the coda, the development, and the final coda, in which we have hitherto found it.

In the *Sonata appassionata*, Op. 57, BEETHOVEN constructs the second theme out of the first by free *contrary motion* of the chief motive:

LISZT, in the *b*-minor Sonata, dedicated to ROBERT SCHUMANN, forms the secondary theme—

325.

by the *augmentation* of the motive marked **a**, of the principal theme :

Allegro energico.

326.

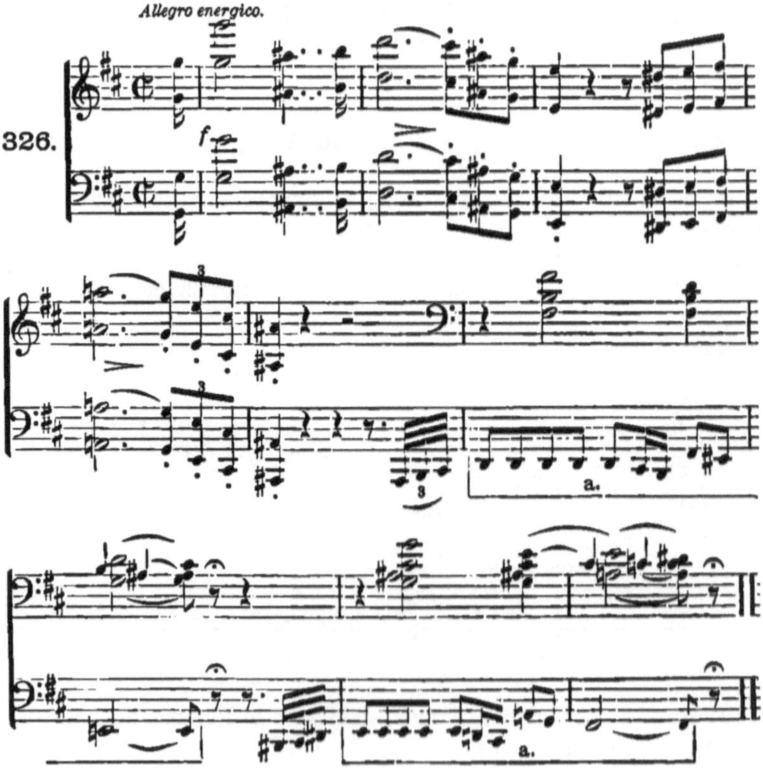

In the *c*-minor Symphony the chief-motive

accompanies all the transformations of the movement.

290. Still, the second theme, as being destined to form the *greatest thematic contrast* of the Sonata-form, is least frequently the place for thematic reminiscence. This is very usual, on the other hand, in the *closing-group*. We have already seen an instance in Mozart's *g*-minor Symphony, in which thematic work occupies part of the closing-group (Fig. 283). In the often-cited *g*-minor Quintet of this master the closing-group consists of the thematic motive and a cadence-formula. The subsequent Coda and connecting-link are also thematic.

291. Thematic relationship of *all* the parts by means of rhythmic similarity is often met with; as, for example, in the *Finale* of BEETHOVEN's *d*-minor Sonata, and in many other works of different composers.

CHAPTER LI.

MODIFICATION OF THE SONATA-FORM IN THE FINALE.

292. The *Finale*, as closing-group of a large work, generally emphasizes from the outset this terminal character by a more decisive manner of closing the several groups of the form. Thus, the first four measures of the Finale of BEETHOVEN's *c*-minor Symphony—

327.

of themselves form as it were a closing-group. So the first theme ends, after a much lengthened half-cadence, with a powerful close on the Tonic:

The *intermediate group*, also, which immediately follows the above with a new motive,

and reaches the key of the reciprocal dominant (see Par. 241, c) by means of a half-cadence, subsequently makes in this key, very perceptibly to the ear, though in livelier rhythm, a perfect cadence and transition to the second theme :

Half-cadence on the Reciprocal Dominant.

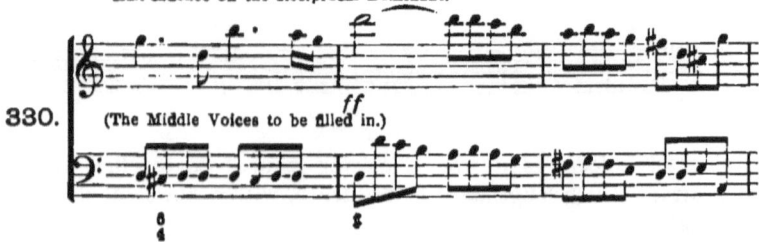

The second theme, too, leads with a very decided cadence into the closing-group,

331.

which latter, on *its* part, in its 9th and 10th measures comes to a perfect tonic close in its key (the Dominant), but on its repetition leads, without cadence, back to the beginning, and the second time to the development.

On account of the exceeding clearness of its construction this movement belongs, together with the Finale of the $c\sharp$-minor Sonata, among the very best models for the young composer. We will observe here, that the $\frac{3}{4}$ meter introduced in the development is a reminiscence of the Scherzo, an episode of the form.

293. It is not unusual, however, for the principal theme of the Finale to have primary form, preferably the small form; as, for example, in MOZART's *g*-minor Symphony (Fig. 40 b). The first movement also exceptionally has small primary form, as in MOZART's *e*-minor Sonata for pianoforte and violin, whose theme is given in Fig. 87, a.

FOURTH PART.

THE HIGHER RONDO-FORMS.

CONCLUSION OF THE WORK.

294. The HIGHER RONDO-FORMS presuppose knowledge and practice of the *Sonata-form*, they being combinations of this form with the *primary form*.

CHAPTER LII.

THE FOURTH RONDO-FORM.

295. The FOURTH RONDO-FORM has for its principal subject a group in two-part or three-part (preferably *two*-part) primary form. This is followed, as in the Sonata, by an episode (intermediate group), mostly short, modulating into the key of, and introducing, the secondary subject. At the close of the secondary subject, closing-group and coda being omitted, follows an episode which leads back to the principal key, and in it repeats the first theme. *Here the first part ends in the principal key.*

Now follows in another key (parallel, subdominant, mediant, homonymic) a *primary form* group, as *second part*, thus taking the place of the *development* in the Sonata.

At the close of this primary form group again enters the episode leading into the principal key, and with it the Reprise, *i. e.*, repetition of the first part without modulation, as in the Sonata-form. (The second theme, therefore, appears in the *principal key*.) As the omission of modulation renders another repetition of the first theme hazardous, the latter is either abridged or its place supplied by a thematically allied free coda.

THIRTY-FOURTH EXERCISE.

Compose, according to these directions and the following examples, some Rondos of the fourth form, as far as possible utilizing previous compositions.

296. The *Finale* of the *A♭-major Sonata* is one of the most notable examples of this kind. The whole movement is in almost continuous motion of sixteenths (interrupted only by short rests) from the beginning. The first theme—

consists of a large period in *A♭*-major, in which is a transient modulation. This period is strictly logically formed by the contraposition and junction of the first and second members of the thesis. Their junction is effected, in fact, after the manner of double counterpoint "in the inversion," the upper voice—

becoming the lower voice :

A short *episode* (4 measures) leads, with the principal motive of the first theme, into the *reciprocal dominant, Bb*-major, which at once becomes the dominant septimachord of the key of *Eb*-major, in which the second theme now enters:

This embraces over 16 measures, and is followed by a transitional passage leading back to the first theme—

which is repeated entire. Its close is immediately followed by a middle group in the key of the mediant—

337.

the first part being repeated. The second part, however, contains no complete phrase, but is composed of four dimeters, by which it modulates into the dominant of *A♭*-major, thence back to the principal theme.

In the Rondo of BEETHOVEN's *C*-major Sonata, Op. 2, the form is more amply developed.

CHAPTER LIII.

THE FIFTH RONDO-FORM.

297. The FIFTH RONDO–FORM is substantially a *Sonata*, in which the place of the *development* is taken by a *large primary form group.*

298. At the close of the first part, however, in many Rondos of this form, the principal theme is repeated in the principal key; in which case a modulation into this key is, of course, necessary. But just as frequently, instead of the repetition in the principal key, is found a Coda in the second key, formed from motives of the first theme. The difference between this and the preceding form is this, that the Rondo of the *fourth* form restricts the Sonata construction to *two themes*, but always repeats the first theme; the Rondo of the *fifth* form, on the contrary, includes every part of the Sonata, but does not always repeat the first theme at the end of the first part.

299. FIRST PART.—The *principal theme* of the fifth Rondo-form is constructed like that of the Sonata, but may have primary form also.

The *episode* (intermediate group) is constructed exactly as in the Sonata, being either thematically reminiscent of the first theme, or independent.

The *second theme* is subject to the same rule of modulation as in the Sonata.

Of the *closing-group* precisely the same is to be said.

The *coda* either recapitulates the first theme by thematic reminiscence, or forms the connecting-link for the repetition of the first theme in the original key. Sometimes the coda is lacking.

The *repetition* of the first theme, when it occurs, is generally in an *abridgment*.

300. SECOND PART.—Now follows, in place of the development, the primary form group specially characteristic of the form, its key-relationship being the same as in the fourth Rondo-form. Not unfrequently this is followed by a bit of actual development, or at least by some kind of thematic work, leading into the

301. THIRD PART, repetition of the first part, without modulation.

302. In the composite large Sonatas these Rondo-forms are found only as closing-groups, and have as such the tendency to a more decided manner of bringing their periods, etc., to a close (see Par. 292).

THIRTY-FIFTH EXERCISE.

Compose, according to these directions and the following examples, Rondos of the fifth form, again preferably utilizing material already on hand.

303. The fifth Rondo-form is exemplified with unusual clearness in BEETHOVEN's Sonata, No. 1, last movement, which accordingly furnishes the best model of this form. The first part comes to a close in Sonata-fashion, ending with a reminiscence of the principal theme.

338.

The dominant septimachord of $A\flat$-major, sounded three times—

suffices to introduce the theme so conclusive for the Rondo-form:

This theme makes in the fifty-first measure a close in $A\flat$-major. Its construction is:

FIRST PART. { Tonic group, complete in itself...................10 measures.
{ Repetition with variations of tone-quality, etc......10   "
Middle group (2 × 4)............................... 8   "
Antithesis 8   "
Middle group and Antithesis repeated as Second
Part (Par. 49)...... 15   "

Total...................51 measures.

We have here, then, *small three-part primary* form, or strictly speaking, in view of the formal structure of the groups, three-part *period-form* (see Chapter VIII), omitting the repetitions, of $10+8+8$ measures.

In the last measure now begins a development with the first motive of the principal subject, leading back in 29 measures to the latter.*

304. The Rondo of the $E\flat$-major Sonata, Op. 7, also belongs to this form. It constructs its second theme with the motive:

the closing-group with:

After the closing-group the principal theme re-enters: *First period:* Thesis, Antithesis (Fig. 26 **b**); *Second period:* Thesis, and— *instead of Antithesis—transition* into c-minor,

---

* But for the song-group in $A\flat$ (Fig. 340) this whole movement would perfectly correspond to the *Finale* of the Sonata-form.

in which key a three-part primary form follows with all its repetitions, then by means of a Coda leads back into the Reprise.

The attention of the young composer is here called to the Rondo of the *Pathetic Sonata* also, which is likewise of the *fifth* form.

CHAPTER LIV.

THE SLOW TEMPO.

305. Thus far the exercises for the Sonata-form and the related large Rondo-forms implied *quick tempo* exclusively. Yet these forms may be applied in *slow* tempo also. The *fifth Rondo-form* might seem, on account of its wealth of material, to make an exception, yet that part of it which is in Sonata-form may be reduced to the dimensions of the *Sonatina*, when it will not be too extended for a slow *tempo*.

306. An example of the fifth Rondo-form in slow time is the celebrated *Largo e mesto* of BEETHOVEN's *D*-major Sonata, Op. 10. The first part is constructed in Sonatina-form:

Second Theme, *a*-minor.

347.

(Ends, after 9 measures, in *a* minor.)

Closing Group.

348.

pp   *cresc.*   *sf*

etc.

(has 4 measures and closes the first part without Coda.)

but the middle group—

349.

p

(Has 14 measures.)

etc.

instead of carrying out the primary form, introduces a new motive :

350.

modulates with it into the dominant of the principal key, and from thence returns to the first theme. Such freedom of abbreviation requires, of course, a slow tempo.

The third part presents, after the regular termination of the Reprise, the closing-group being omitted, a magnificent thematically figurated elaboration of the principal motive (Fig. 345), leading, with

the figure 🎵 of the middle group, to the close. This thematic

work may be regarded either as repetition, after the Rondo manner, of the principal theme, or as Coda in the sense of Paragraphs 287, 288.

To the close is attached a Coda of very impressive character, thematically reminiscent of the motive | a | in Fig. 345.

307. *Sonata*-form (or, as the case may be, Sonatina-form) is found in the slow movements of our classical composers *very often*. But in consideration of the *tempo* they almost always reduce the development portion to a minimum, or do away with it entirely, satisfying the need of thematic work by the variations of the principal theme.

308. A Sonata-movement in slow tempo *without* development is illustrated by the *Adagio molto* of BEETHOVEN'S *c*-minor Sonata, Op. 10.

351.

After the regular close of the first part in $E\flat$-major, a single septimachord suffices to lead into the regularly closing Reprise:

352

309. In the *d*-minor Sonata, Op. 31, is found the same form. The *intermediate group* begins thus:

353.

and makes the regular close on the reciprocal dominant, *C*-major. Here the second theme enters in the key of the dominant, *F*-major,

354

and constitutes a two-part period of the third form (Par. 37, 38). This is followed—closing-group and coda being omitted—by a connecting-link of four measures leading to the Reprise, in which everything takes its regular course, but the principal theme is varied by a lively figuration in thirty-second notes.

Compare here, also, the *Andante* of MOZART's *F*-major Sonata, whose principal subject is given in Fig. 262.

310. Sonata-form with *short* development is shown in the *Adagio affettuoso ed appassionato* of BEETHOVEN's *F*-major string-quartet, Op. 18.

311. On the other hand, the *Adagio molto e mesto* of BEETHOVEN'S grand *F*-major quartet, Op. 59, exhibits sonata-form with *large* development. The principal theme, whose thesis here follows (in the antithesis the melody is taken by the 'cello), has large period-form.

355.

The intermediate group takes its cue from the last motive of the theme,—

356.

in four measures reaches the reciprocal dominant, *G*-major, makes in three measures a half-cadence on it twice, and a transition to *c*-minor; in which the second theme now enters in the 'cello.

After thirteen measures this theme makes a preparation of the close, thus:

but here is constructed a closing formula so significant and peculiar that it may be regarded as special closing-group, even though its beginning coincides with the formation of the secondary subject:

(repeated with slightly varied figuration.)

Whether the subsequent five measures are to be reckoned in the closing-group, or regarded, entirely or partly, as Coda, is immaterial. But now begins the *development*, which has 38 measures against 45 of the first part, and is occupied first with the second theme, then with the first, and finally with the closing-group. From the latter is developed a thought in D♭-major—*Molto cantabile*—of great tenderness, forming as it were an *episode of the Sonata-form*, such as often occurs in the development, viz:

360.

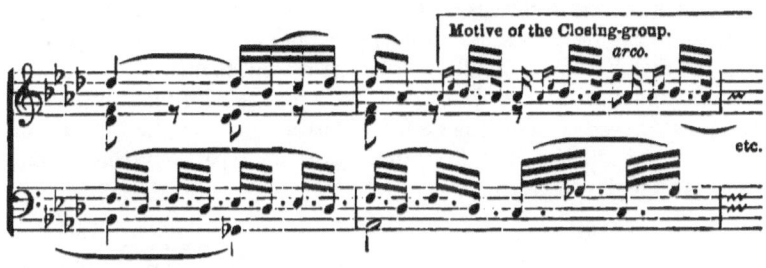

The 'cello now continues, leading with the first motive through the circle of Fifths—*Db*-major, *Ab*-major, *eb*-minor, *bb*-minor, *f*-minor, *C*-major—to the dominant of the principal key, when the closing formula is repeated and transition is made into the Reprise. This latter takes the regular course. At its close, however, enters (as not seldom happens in the slow movement in Sonata-form) a repetition of the principal theme (which repetition was omitted at the beginning of the Reprise). This repetition leads to a very elaborate figurated cadenza, which introduces the next movement of the quartet (Thème Russe, *Allegro*.)

312. Another very noteworthy instance of the application of the Sonata-form in the slow movement is the *Andante* of MOZART'S great *C*-major symphony, which movement shows, not only in its totality, but also in all its separate parts, an extremely interesting metrical construction. The principal subject ends in the eleventh measure, and in the same measure begins to repeat itself (see Paragraph 232), forming a thesis of 8 measures with half-cadence on the dominant—the *C*-major Triad,—indicated by the numeral V in the following figure. Hereupon abruptly enters, in the key of *c-minor,* a theme which must be regarded as episode (intermediate group) ;

861.

it makes, after eight measures of bold and striking harmony, a half-
cadence on the *reciprocal dominant* (*G*-major) of the key of the movement (*F*-major).   This is followed by the second theme, of 12⌣ measures, in the key of the Dominant, to which a closing-group of 4
measures succeeds.   There is no Coda, but a figure for the first violin
serves as a transition, the first time into the repetition, the second
time into the development:

362.

etc.

The scheme of the movement is continued as follows.—The intermediate group or link-episode is lengthened to the extent of 14 measures.
The principal theme is thematically elaborated with the figurated
motive in 32d-notes, which accompanied its repetition in the first part.
This motive is worked up to a fiery *ff*, which leads, with a reminiscence of the intermediate group,

363.   *f*   *p*

now not into the principal subject, but into the secondary one, which
latter thus begins here the third part of the Sonata-form.   After this
everything follows regularly, *but*—after the closing-group comes the
repetition—omitted above—of the principal theme.   A Coda of 3
measures brings the whole to an end.

THIRTY–SIXTH EXERCISE.

Compose a slow movement in Sonata-form or higher Rondo-form.

CHAPTER LV.

THE COMPOSITE LARGE SONATA.

313.   A composite piece of music for the pianoforte, or for the
pianoforte and a single solo instrument, is generally called Sonata
when its first movement has Sonata-form.   A composition in the same
form for orchestra is called SYMPHONY, for a union of string-instru-
ments, etc., QUARTET, QUINTET, etc.   Accordingly, RAFF's *g*-minor
Suite, Op. 162, might also be named Sonata, as its first movement is
in that form, though with modern modifications.

314.   The *key* of a Sonata is determined by the *first movement*, not
by the *introduction*, if it have one; the KREUTZER-Sonata, therefore, is
in *a*-minor.   In many Sonatas (Symphonies, Quartets) in *minor* the
Finale is in the major mode of the same key, instances of which are
BEETHOVEN's *c*-minor Symphony, *d*-minor (ninth) Symphony.

315.   An *Adagio*, even of large dimensions, but leading directly
into the *Allegro*, is regarded—not as a separate movement, but—as
introduction to the *Allegro*, which latter ranks as *first* movement.
Such an *Adagio* precedes, for example, the often-quoted *e*-minor Sonatina by MOZART (see Fig. 49 a),—

364.

and after more than 38 measures in large three-part primary form makes a half-cadence and leads into the *Allegro*, which is in Sonatina-form. Every one is familiar with the *Grave* which introduces the Pathetic Sonata and frequently interrupts the *Allegro*. The first movement of the *A*-major Symphony, too, is preceded by an *Adagio* of considerable dimensions;

365.

and the same is to be said of MOZART's *E♭*-major Symphony and of many of HAYDN's Symphonies. The introduction to BEETHOVEN's great *C*-major quartet is well known.

316. Sonatas of but *one movement*, in Sonata-form, occur, but very rarely.

317. Sonatas of *two movements* are of frequent occurrence. An instance *with large introduction* is MOZART's *e*-minor Sonatina already so often quoted, in which the Sonata-form movement is followed by a Rondo of the third form, properly a Minuet with two Trios.

366.

First Trio. Second Theme.

Second Trio. Third Theme.

The same master's (Duo-) Sonata, No. 4, in *G*-major, also consists of two movements, the second being a theme with variations.

318. Sonatas of two movements *without introduction* are, *e. g.*, Mozart's other *e*-minor (Duo-) Sonata (see Fig. 31, **b**), Haydn's *c♯*-minor piano-sonata,

367.

with Minuet in *c♯*-minor, *C♯*-major. By Beethoven, for instance, the Sonatinas, Op. 49, the Sonatas, Op. 54, Op. 101 (*E*-major); the great *C*-major Sonata, Op. 53, also has only two movements, for the *Adagio* inserted between Sonata and Rondo is to be regarded as merely the introduction to the latter.

319. Most Sonatas have *three movements*, among them the most noted, as the Pathetic, the *c♯*-minor, the Appassionata. In the *c♯*-minor Sonata the *last* movement only has Sonata-form, the first movement belongs to no special form, for which reason Beethoven has inscribed this Sonata as "*quasi una fantasia.*"

320. The *perfect* Large Sonata-form, as found in most of Haydn's and Mozart's Symphonies (in all the later ones), in all of Beethoven's Symphonies, in the large string-quartets and quintets and kindred species of instrumental music, consists of *four movements*, viz.:

> an *Allegro*, with or without introduction ;
> a *slow movement ;*
> a *Minuet* or *Scherzo ;* and
> a *Finale, Allegro·*

321. By way of exception the 2d and 3d movements change places, *e. g.*, in the Ninth Symphony and the *B♭*-major Sonata, Op. 106, for the reason that the great dimensions and the thematic character of the first movements require the contrast which is thus afforded. The place of the slow movement is sometimes taken by an *Allegretto* as in BEETHOVEN's *E♭*-major Sonata, Op. 31, in his 7th and 8th Symphonies. On the other hand, the *Minuet* in the 8th Symphony is *slow*, in the graceful and ceremonious movement originally characteristic of this dance. Exceptions like these result from, and are justifiable only by, exceptional conditions. To introduce them from mere caprice would be to betray ignorance of the essence of formal construction, and a desire to help one's self out by recourse to what is unessential and external. That movements are sometimes joined with others which happen to be already written—a procedure which, generally, of course excludes logical unity,—is neither to be denied nor to be absolutely condemned. Such combinations have at least the unity of the author's individuality, which is by no means to be undervalued.

322. There are exceptional cases of the Sonata (so called) *without a single movement in Sonata-form*, as, for instance, BEETHOVEN's *A♭*-major Sonata, Op. 26, which consists of Variations, Scherzo, Funeral March and Rondo.

THIRTY–SEVENTH EXERCISE.

Combine movements already composed into Sonatas, with a view to subsequent filling up.

CHAPTER LVI.

OTHER APPLICATIONS OF THE INSTRUMENTAL FORMS.

323. The great masters of our classical instrumental music and their contemporaries and followers were so familiar with the principal form of that kind of music—the Sonata-form—that they brought into view its characteristic qualities in their larger *vocal* compositions also. Here the given text, by its logical and psychological import, of course set limits to their purely musical inclination. Yet we find those characteristic qualities not only in the Masses of HAYDN and MOZART, but also in the domain of the Opera. The $B\flat$-major aria of Ottavio in "Don Giovanni" ("il mio tesoro intanto") has the structure of the Sonatina, as also the entrance-aria of Elvira (in the same opera), marked as a trio on account of the little episodes of Don Giovanni and Leporello:

368.

Ah! chi mi di - ce ma - i,

Elvira's second grand aria,

369.

Mi tra - di   quell' alma in - gra - ta,

is a Rondo of the first form; Pizarro's aria in "Fidelio" has Sonata-form. But especially the outset of the Sonata-form (from the principal theme to the entrance of the secondary one) is found in numerous accompanied vocal compositions (even *ensemble* pieces) which involve a *dramatic* scene.

324. That the *Overtures* of our classical masters belong almost exclusively to the Sonata-form may at this point be assumed as already

known.   Also the *Allegro* of WAGNER's "Tannhäuser" Overture
(which is constructed from motives of the Venusberg scene) belongs
to this form, which in a certain sense is extended to a Rondo of the
fifth form by the middle group in *G*-major:

MEYERBEER's Overture to "Struensee," in its construction strongly
suggestive of BEETHOVEN's "Egmont" Overture, has also Sonata-
form.

The great composers of the French and Italian opera, BOIELDIEU,
AUBER, ROSSINI, BELLINI, etc., likewise avail themselves of this form,
in the sharp outlines of the several divisions relatively to each other.

The Overtures of GLUCK, who flourished *before* the development
of the instrumental forms, do not, indeed, exhibit the sharply defined
Sonata-form, though they give unmistakable indications of it.

325. The tendency of the opera in our time, however, has led
through inner necessity to the substitution of the *Prelude* (Vorspiel)
in place of the Overture.   No finer example of the operatic Prelude
can be had than the introduction to WAGNER's "Lohengrin."   MAX
BRUCH's Prelude to his "Loreley" is also worthy of note in this connection.

We have followed up and practised form-structure, from the simplest combination of but two measures, in the so-called Section or
Dimeter, to the splendid art-fabric of the grand Sonata and its kindred

forms.   In so doing we have seen spread out before us an almost inexhaustible wealth of material.   Here, therefore, as in the other branches of musical construction, in order to attain to finished art-creations such as we have had repeated occasion to contemplate, over and above natural talent the most thorough *practical knowledge* is requisite, since this alone will enable us, in the midst of this *embarras de richesses,* to lay hold of that which alone can be esthetically (artistically) the right thing, on every occasion, without fear of error.

APPENDIX.

THE STROPHE.

FOLLOWING an analogy of music to poetry, some modern writers on musical subjects have applied the term STROPHE to certain groups varying in extent, whose construction does not strictly fall under any of the regular forms. Thus, the celebrated editor of pianoforte literature, the late DR. THEODORE KULLAK, in his Instructive Edition of CHOPIN'S Works,* distinguishes in some of the Nocturnes "larger divisions, which are related to each other, not like chief and secondary subjects, for example, but rather like the Strophes of a poem; for while they are indeed specifically *different* in point of *contents*, they serve nevertheless to express *one and the same fundamental mood*," etc., etc. Of the Nocturne in *B*-major, Op. 9, No. 3, he says that in its chief subject "three special parts may be distinguished, which in a certain sense form its Strophes. These Strophes are indeed *different*, but not essentially *unlike*, in point of contents, and they constantly alternate with each other," etc. He divides the chief subject thus:

1st Part or Strophe			....	measures	1—12.
2d	"	"	....	"	13—20.
1st	"	"	(repeated)............	"	21—32.
2d	"	"	(repeated)............	"	33—40.
3d	"	"	....	"	41—56.
2d	"	"	(repeated)............	"	57—64.
3d	"	"	(repeated)............	"	65—80.
2d	"	"	(repeated)............	"	81—87.

Of the Nocturne in *Db*-major, Op. 27, No. 2, DR. KULLAK says that it "divides best into Strophes, for it does not develop into groups of parallel subjects, in the strict sense. Even the bass moves from begin-

---

* Edited in English by Albert R. Parsons; G. Schirmer, publisher.

ning to end in homogeneous figures. I have assumed eight Strophes, which afford variety of shading, without offering essentially new contents. The chief Strophes are the Ist, IId and VIIIth." His division into Strophes is the following :

Strophe   I..measures 2— 9.
"   II...   "   10—13.
"   III (transposed repetition of II)...........   "   14—25.
"   IV (repetition of I)........................ .   "   26—33.
"   V (transposed repetition of II)...........   "   34—45.
"   VI (repetition of I)......................   "   46—53.
"   VII (repetition of II).....................   "   53—62.
"   VIII (real *Coda* of the piece)..............   "   62—Fine.

The Nocturne in *B*-major, Op. 32, No. 1, is thus divided :

Strophe I.............................measures 1— 8.
Interlude........... ....   "   8—12.
Strophe I (repeated)........... ....   "   13—20.
Strophe II ....   "   21—30.
Interlude.................................. "   31—41.
Strophe II (repeated).....................   "   42—51.
Interlude.................................. "   52—61.
Coda....................................... "   62—Fine.

RUDOLPH WESTPHAL, in his "Allgemeine Theorie der Musikalischen Rhythmik," applies the word Strophe, in a *composite* sense, to a somewhat large sub-division of a composition. The first 48 measures of the first movement (*Allegro*) of BEETHOVEN's Sonata, No. 1 (*f*-minor), for instance, form, according to him, a composite Strophe, made of nine simple Strophes, thus:

1st Strophe............... ....measures 1— 8.
2d   "   ....   "   8—16.
3d   "   ....   "   16—18.
4th   "   .... "   18—20.
5th   "   .... "   20—25.
6th   "   ....   "   26—30.
7th   "   ....   "   31—36.
8th   "   ....   "   37—41.
9th   "   ....   "   41—48.

The same author divides the whole of the *Adagio Cantabile* of BEETHOVEN's Pathetic Sonata into two composite Strophes, according to the following scheme :

STROPHE I.

1st Simple Strophe,—two 4-measure Periods,*........measures 1— 8.
2d   "   "   —Repetition (varied)..............   "   9—16.
3d   "   "   —5-measure Period..............   "   17—23.
4th   "   "   —Periods ....   "   24—28.
5th   "   "   —Repetition of 1st Strophe ....   *   29—36.

STROPHE II.

6th Simple Strophe,—two 4-measure Periods.........measures 37—44.
7th   "   "   —6-measure Period ....   "   45—50.
8th   "   "   —Repetition of 1st Strophe........   "   51—58.
9th   "   "   —Repetition of 2d Strophe........   "   59—66.
10th "   "   —(Coda).......................   "   66—Fine.

---

* On the ground that it is a perversion, based on misconception, of the ancient Greek rhythmical theory, which he holds to be the only correct one even for modern music, WESTPHAL rejects the commonly received doctrine, first formulated by ANTOINE REICHA (1770—1836), with regard to the structure of the musical Period.

INDEX.

www.ingramcontent.com/pod-product-compliance
Lightning Source LLC
Chambersburg PA
CBHW031345020726
47499CB00005B/1410